COMPOSITION:

Prewriting, Response, Revision

LITERATURE-BASED EDITION

Sharon Sorenson

Dedicated to serving

AMSCO

our nation's youth

AMSCO SCHOOL PUBLICATIONS, INC.
315 Hudson Street / New York, N.Y. 10013

As an English teacher and department chair in Indiana, **Sharon Sorenson** has taught thousands of students and hundreds of teachers. She has also taught at the University of Evansville and written eleven books for students and teachers. She is presently a full-time writer, lecturer, and in-service instructor for high school teachers.

When ordering this book, please specify either **R 603 W**
or COMPOSITION: PREWRITING, RESPONSE, REVISION, LITERATURE-BASED EDITION

ISBN 1-56765-007-4

Printed in the United States of America

1 2 3 4 5 6 7 8 9 10   99 98 97 96 95 94 93

Contents

To the Teacher

he goal of this book is to use literature-based instruction to help students improve their ability to write a composition of three or four paragraphs.

Each of the ten units consists of the following sections:

PREWRITING

Each prewriting activity begins with a literary selection. Open-ended questions help students respond to the literature, and students are asked to keep a response journal in which to record their thoughts, an activity designed to direct students toward content and to guide them to think about a topic they will write about. An active reading segment directs students' attention to a single writing technique modeled in the literature and emphasized in the unit. The technique addresses syntactic fluency and verbal deftness, preparing students with a complex of writing skills to bring to bear in the writing of a specific composition.

RESPONSE

By referring to their journal responses and applying writing techniques in a modeling sequence, students are prepared to write the first draft of a composition suggested by the literature selection. They are given help and guidance in formulating the content, in organizing and developing their thoughts. Narrative, descriptive, and expository modes are included in the ten units.

REVISION

Students are prepared for a revision of their first draft. Each unit emphasizes an organization-development technique and a means for maintaining coherence, both of which are followed by modeling sequences referring students to the literary selection and to their own works in progress.

Students are also shown two common errors to watch for in proofreading their compositions. By relying on peer editors and self-evaluation processes, students complete a final draft.

A key feature of this book is that it reflects the best research and methodology: the teaching of composition is integrated and literature-based. The literature provides both writing models and springboards for thought; and the integration guarantees that the many strands of instruction involved in the complex act of writing a composition are woven together as they are directed toward the culminating act of formulating subject matter, organization, and development. In addition, to reflect the modern writer's environment, computer hints are included throughout the text (three or four in each unit) which suggest means by which students can use the technology to improve their writing skills.

Acknowledgments

Grateful acknowledgment is made to the following sources for permission to use copyrighted materials, which appear in this book on the pages indicated in italics:

BBC Publications: *156–158*, from *The Ascent of Man* by J. Bronowski. Published by BBC Publications, 1973 (for Canadian rights).

Chatto and Windus Ltd.: *130–133*, "The Lottery Ticket," from *The Wife and Other Stories* in THE TALES OF TCHEKOV, translated by Constance Garnett. Reprinted by permission of the translator's literary estate and Chatto and Windus Ltd. (for Canadian rights).

Current History, Inc.: *113–114*, from "Crime and Violence in American Life" by Robert K. Woetzel, October, 1968, *Current History.*

Don James: *50–52*, "Chicken!" from *Girls and Gangs* by Don James. Copyright © 1963 by Don James. Included by permission of the author and his agents, Lenniger Literary Agency, Inc., New York.

Little, Brown and Company: *156–158*, adapted from "Gold" from *The Ascent of Man* by J. Bronowski. Copyright © 1973 by J. Bronowski. By permission of Little, Brown and Company.

Macmillan Publishing Co., Inc.: *130–133*, "The Lottery Ticket," reprinted with permission of Macmillan Publishing Co., Inc., from *The Wife and Other Stories* by Anton Chekhov, translated from the Russian by Constance Garnett. Copyright 1918 by Macmillan Publishing Co., Inc., renewed 1946 by Constance Garnett.

The New Yorker: *2*, "Calcutta Weather" from "The Talk of the Town," copyright © 1978, *The New Yorker*, reprinted by permission. *177–179*, "A Friendly Product" by John Brooks, copyright © 1979 by John Brooks in *The New Yorker*, reprinted by permission.

The New York Times: *15–16*, "Thesaurus, at 200, Still Looks for (Seeks) Words," by Herbert Mitgang, January 18, 1979. Copyright © 1979 by The New York Times Company, reprinted by permission.

Random House, Inc.: *69–70*, excerpted from "A Ride Through Spain" by Truman Capote. Copyright 1950 by Truman Capote, reprinted from *Selected Writings of Truman Capote*, by permission of Random House, Inc. Originally appeared in *The New Yorker.*

Saturday Review: *90–91*, "What Do We Do About Television?" by Nicholas Johnson. Copyright © 1970 by *Saturday Review*, all rights reserved, reprinted with permission.

Ziff-Davis Publishing Company: *31–32*, excerpted from "Friendship: An Inquiry" from p. 65 of *Psychology Today Magazine*. Copyright © 1979 by Ziff-Davis Publishing Company.

COMPOSITION:

Prewriting, Response, Revision

Unit 1

A Description
of a Weather Experience

PREWRITING

Reading the Literature

Everyone has experienced extremes of weather. As you read to enjoy the three literary excerpts which follow, look for clues about the writer's reaction to the weather phenomenon described. Try to imagine how each writer felt about his or her experiences.

First read this short passage by Joseph Conrad describing a ship, the *Nan-Shan*, caught in a typhoon at sea.

> The sea, flattened down in the heavier gusts, would uprise and overwhelm both ends of the *Nan-Shan* in snowy rushes of foam, expanding wide, beyond both sails, into the night. And on this dazzling sheet, spread under the blackness of the clouds and emitting a bluish glow, Captain MacWhirr could catch a desolate glimpse of a few tiny specks black as ebony, the tops of the hatches, the battened companions, the heads of the covered winches, the foot of a mast.
>
> from *Typhoon*

Now read another passage by a master writer, Mark Twain.

> I had myself called with the four-o'clock watch, mornings, for one cannot see too many summer sunrises on the Mississippi. They are enchanting. First, there is the eloquence of silence; for a deep hush broods everywhere. Next, there is the haunting sense of loneliness, isolation, remoteness from the worry and bustle of the world. The dawn creeps in stealthily; the solid walls

of black forest soften to gray, and vast stretches of the river open up and reveal themselves; the water is glass-smooth, gives off spectral little wreaths of white mist; there is not the faintest breath of wind, nor stir of leaf; the tranquillity is profound and infinitely satisfying. Then a bird pipes up, another follows, and soon the pipings develop into a jubilant riot of music. You see none of the birds; you simply move through an atmosphere of song, which seems to sing itself. When the light has become a little stronger, you have one of the fairest and softest pictures imaginable. You have the intense green of the massed and crowded foliage nearby; you see it paling shade by shade in front of you; upon the next projecting cape, a mile off or more, the tint has lightened to the tender young green of spring; the cape beyond that one has almost lost color, and the furthest one, miles away under the horizon, sleeps upon the water, a mere dim vapor, and hardly separable from the sky above it and about it. And all this stretch of river is a mirror, and you have the shadowy reflections of the leafage and the curving shores and the receding capes pictured in it. Well, that is all beautiful; soft and rich and beautiful; and when the sun gets well up, and distributes a pink flush here and a powder of gold yonder and a purple haze where it will yield the best effect, you grant that you have seen something that is worth remembering.

from *Life on the Mississippi*

Finally, read the following article from *The New Yorker* depicting another writer's experience with the weather.

On Wednesday, the twenty-seventh of September, the Calcutta morning papers came out with these forecasts from the government's meteorological observatory: "Occasional rain," "One or two showers," "Occasional rain or thundershowers." Even before the papers were distributed, Calcutta was awash in torrential rains, and much of it was lying under a sheet of water, with no trams, no buses, no telephones, no electricity, no drinking water. Soon a bore tide in the Hooghly River, on which Calcutta lies, and backflow from sewers and drains further inundated the city, submerging some streets under as much as fifteen feet of water. (It was rumored that rats and snakes were swimming around in the main thoroughfares.) The rain, accompanied by strong winds, continued to lash the city, and within thirty-six hours there was a rainfall of forty centimeters—the heaviest in sixty years. And this deluge was just part of four successive floods, over a period of two months, in Calcutta, in West Bengal, and, indeed, in much of northern India.

Reader Response

After reading these three excerpts which relate weather experiences, think about some experience you have had with extreme weather. You have probably experienced a blizzard, a disastrous rainfall, a powerful windstorm, a spell of intense heat or bitter cold, or prolonged drought. At the other extreme, you must have enjoyed a spell of weather so perfect and beautiful as to be unforgettable. In your response journal, freewrite for fifteen minutes about some experience you have had with extreme weather. The term "freewrite" means to write freely, without restrictions, to write without stopping, without judging correctness of spelling, sentence structure, or grammar, jotting down whatever comes to your mind about your topic. There is only one rule for freewriting: keep your pen or pencil moving, even if you rewrite the same phrase a couple of times. Freewriting may be a series of phrases, even lists of words, and will not necessarily appear in paragraph form.

COMPUTER HINT

If you work at a computer, freewrite at the keyboard for fifteen minutes.

If you plan to do all of your response journal entries at the keyboard, you may want to create a separate journal file. Next, be sure to create subfiles so that you can find specific prewriting materials quickly. For instance, you may want to list this entry as "journal.wea" to remind you that this entry is your response to weather descriptions. Be sure to print a copy of your entry for your folder and save the text on disk as well.

Active Reading

Look again at the three literary selections. How do you think each of the three writers above felt about his or her experiences? What words or phrases gave you clues about their feelings? Underline those key words or phrases and make notes in the margins about what clues these terms give about the writers' feelings.

Studying Model Writing Techniques

Picture-making Words

REMEMBER! All sorts of choices are open to you in the kinds of words and sentences you use to express yourself.

The choices you make in the kinds of words and sentences you use determine what we refer to as "style." The exercises which follow will give you training in making these choices. By applying to your own writing what you learn from these exercises, you will develop a more personal, expressive writing style.

The following examples, most from the literary selections, illustrate how the writers use picture-making words. These words have the power to make pictures because they appeal concretely to the senses:

EXACT COLOR:	ebony, gray, pink, scarlet
EXACT SHAPE:	rectangular, spiral, crescent
EXACT SIZE:	speck, hulk, puny, mile
EXACT SOUND:	whisper, belch, piping, hush
EXACT TOUCH OR TEXTURE:	bristles, powder, vapor, sandpaper

Exercise 1   List below five exact, picture-making words or phrases used by Conrad to create a powerful description.

1. _____
2. _____
3. _____
4. _____
5. _____

Exercise 2   List below ten exact, picture-making words or phrases used by Twain to create a powerful description.

1. _____
2. _____
3. _____
4. _____
5. _____
6. _____
7. _____
8. _____
9. _____
10. _____

Exercise 3   List below eight picture-making words or phrases used in *The New Yorker* article to create a powerful description.

1. _____
2. _____
3. _____
4. _____
5. _____
6. _____
7. _____
8. _____

Exercise 4 Here are ten lists of picture-making words. Add at least one appropriate word of your own to each list; try for two wherever you can.

1. *Color*
   maroon
   cobalt   _____
   leaden
   peach   _____

2. *Whiteness*
   silver
   alabaster   _____
   ivory
   foam   _____

3. *Container*
   pitcher
   vase   _____
   flask
   vial   _____

4. *Light*
   phosphorescent
   spark   _____
   torch
   dawn   _____

5. *Bigness*
   towering
   hulk   _____
   bloated
   Goliath   _____

6. *Smallness*
   molecule
   pygmy   _____
   gnat
   petite   _____

7. *Shape*
   parallel
   hairpin   _____
   coil
   wisp   _____

8. *Texture*
   satin
   wax   _____
   pebbly
   dough   _____

9. *Sound*
   rasp
   blare   _____
   drone
   gasp   _____

10. *Ugliness*
    maggot
    mutilated   _____
    garbage
    smeared   _____

Exercise 5 Try writing five original sentences. In each sentence, use at least two picture-making words from any of the preceding lists. First, study the two examples that follow. Then write your own sentences. You may change the form of the picture-making words you choose from the lists.

Examples: a. The *alabaster* moon floated in a *cobalt* sky.
             b. *Parallel* tracks of *silver foam* marked our course on the flat, *leaden* sea.

1. _____

   _____

2. _____

   _____

3. _____

4. _____

_____

5. _____

_____

With these prewriting activities behind you, you are ready to write your first draft of a description of a weather experience.

RESPONSE

Modeling

Think about the picture-making words you found in the three selections above. Turn to your response journal in which you wrote about an experience you have had with memorable weather. Look for picture-making words or phrases you have used. Add others where you can, to show color, shape, size, sound, smell, touch, or texture—words that will give details similar to the kinds included in the three models.

Writing

Now that you have added picture-making details to your journal entry, use it as a basis by which to begin your first draft. Consider these suggestions:

In your first paragraph, you may wish to sketch the background of the weather event you are going to describe. You can tell about the circumstances, the time, the place, and the people involved. In beginning this paragraph, you will also be introducing your composition. Try to write an introduction that will not only lead into your subject, but will also be interesting, perhaps by setting up some surprise or suspense. The following examples may give you some ideas.

    a. The date was January 15. The place was Chicago. It was a day that seemed to begin like any other day.

    b. It is true that snow had been predicted. It is true that everyone made the usual preparations with boots, warm clothing, snow tires, and shovels.

    c. Most people favor spring. The poets praise spring. Lovers and golfers wait for spring. I dissent.

In the second paragraph, you may wish to write a vivid description of the weather experience itself. Try to build up a powerful impact by giving many details. Use picture-making words of color, shape, size, and feel. (You may wish to devote two paragraphs to your description.)

In your final paragraph, tell about the results or aftermath of the extreme weather. You may wish to concentrate on the general results as they affected the land and many people. Or you may wish to concentrate on how the weather affected you personally, and on what you thought and felt about your experiences.

In this first draft, concentrate on the subject matter: your main ideas and their supporting details. Later you will revise and polish.

REVISION

Now that you have completed the first draft of your description of a weather experience, you are ready to revise. In the revision process, we will focus on organization, chains of meaning, and proofreading details. Use these materials as a model for your own revision process.

Checking Organization

Unity

REMEMBER! Organized thinking is essential in composition writing.

One important aspect of organization is unity. Unity means that in each sentence, paragraph, and composition you write, your thoughts do not wander illogically.

For instance, in *Typhoon*, Conrad unifies the piece with words that show struggle: *gusts, uprise, overwhelm, rushes*. Of sunrises, Twain shows unity in his description with words like *enchanting, eloquence, haunting, isolation, remoteness, stealthily, spectral*, and *tranquillity*. The *New Yorker* article unifies thoughts with words and phrases like *awash, torrential, sheet of water, bore tide, backflow, inundated, submerging*, and *deluge*.

The following exercise will help you learn to recognize unity of thought.

Exercise 6   In each of the following groups, one item does not belong. Circle the item that does not belong. In the space provided, explain briefly why the item you have circled does not belong in the group. The first one has been done for you as an example.

1. blizzard, cyclone, gale, hurricane, (shelter,) typhoon

   A shelter is not a storm, as all the others are.

2. automobile, bed, chair, dresser, sofa, table

   _____

3. eating, farming, laughing, breathing, talking, thinking

   _____

4. briefcase, jacket, shirt, shoes, slacks, tie

   _____

5. crash, explosion, float, roar, scream, thunder

_____

6. chisel, file, hammer, saw, screwdriver, wood

_____

7. bookkeeping, copying, filing, mailing, traveling, typing

_____

8. baseball, basketball, energy, football, hockey, soccer

_____

9. anger, fear, joy, memory, sadness, worry

_____

10. clapping, grasping, hammering, running, sewing, writing

_____

11. comma, exclamation point, paragraph, period, quotation marks, semicolon

_____

12. cocoa, gasoline, juice, milk, tea, water

_____

13. blush, frown, hate, smile, sneer, stare

_____

14. gallop, jog, stumble, run, sprint, trot

_____

15. honor, integrity, loyalty, envy, truth, trust

_____

Modeling

Skim the three literary selections at the beginning of this unit. Notice that every detail, every word, helps the writer convey the description. In other words, the selections maintain unity.

Read your own work in progress. Do all of the details belong to your narration of a weather experience? Ask a peer editor for his or her response. Cross out any ideas which wander illogically and thereby destroy the unity of your essay.

Checking Chains of Meaning

Transition Words and Phrases

REMEMBER! In composition writing, sentences are not individual or isolated. Instead, the thought is carried along from sentence to sentence in a chain of meaning.

Transition words and phrases act as links in the chain of meaning of sentence sequences. The following are examples of transition words and phrases:

however	as a result	moreover	then
nevertheless	therefore	besides	next
on the contrary	thus	that is	instead
consequently	in summary	in addition	

Exercise 7 Pick one of the literary selections on pages 1–2. Circle the transition words and phrases which act as links in the chain of meaning.

Exercise 8 Provide a transition word or phrase that fits most appropriately in each of the following sentence sequences.

1. She knew there was danger on the job. _____, she decided to become a police officer.

2. First, the soil is carefully prepared. _____, the tulip bulbs are planted.

3. The mouse could not resist the alluring cheese. _____, it was caught in the trap.

4. The trains are crowded and dirty; _____, they are seldom on time.

5. The movie was expected to flop at the box office. _____, it turned out to be one of the biggest hits of all time.

6. The furniture appeared to be expensive. _____, the color scheme was atrocious. _____, there wasn't a comfortable chair in the apartment.

7. It had not rained for weeks. _____, the crops were threatened. _____, there was a serious danger of forest fires.

8. Most of the people ate in the company cafeteria. _____, some preferred to bring their own lunch. _____, there were those few dieters who skipped the midday meal altogether.

9. The boss was thought to be humorless and stern. _____, he was actually human, considerate, and fair.

10. Arthur had one ambition. _____, he wanted to marry a woman with an independent career.

Exercise 9 In each sentence sequence below, you are given only the transition word or phrase of the last sentence. Complete that sentence with words of your own that continue the chain of meaning. The first is done for you as an example.

1. She wanted to buy a car. However, *she feared the rising cost of gasoline.*
   _____

2. The jogger felt she could not run another step. Nevertheless, _____
   _____

3. The roads were covered with ice. Consequently, _____

   _____

4. Once inexpensive, fish has soared in price. Therefore, _____

   _____

5. There are many ways to improve television broadcasting. For example, _____

   _____

6. They decided not to stay at the beach. It was mobbed with people. Besides, _____

   _____

7. Black clouds filled the sky. The air was still. Then, _____

   _____

8. He kept me on the phone practically forever. As a result, _____

   _____

9. The ads lead consumers to think that cola drinks are a refreshing and healthful way
   to quench their thirst. On the contrary, _____

   _____

10. Columbus set out to find a passage to India. Instead, _____

    _____

Modeling

Reread your writing in progress. Check to see if your thoughts are carried along from sentence to sentence in a chain of meaning. If possible, ask a peer or peers to check, too. Add transition words and phrases as needed to move your thoughts smoothly along through the paragraph.

Proofreading

The final step in revising is proofreading—checking the grammar, usage, and mechanics details. Two common errors are emphasized for your attention: sentence fragments and redundancy. The exercises that follow will help you to recognize and avoid these errors in your writing.

Eliminating Sentence Fragments

You know that some groups of words are sentences. You also know that, in our writing system, you begin a sentence with a capital letter and end it with a period (or a question mark or exclamation point when appropriate).

Other groups of words, usually clauses and phrases, also form a kind of unit of meaning, but they cannot stand alone as a sentence and should not be written as a sentence.

In writing the first draft of a composition, we concentrate mainly on the thought of what is being said. It is fairly common to make an occasional sentence-fragment error by writing a clause or phrase as though it were a sentence.

Refresh your mind with the exercises that follow. Note that you cannot tell a sentence fragment from a sentence by length. A sentence can be short. A fragment can be long.

Exercise 10   Five of the following are sentences; five are sentence fragments. Place an X next to the sentence fragments.

_____ **1.** Wood floats.

_____ **2.** From the first day of that week to the last.

_____ **3.** As if they were gulls soaring on air currents, the gliders floated through space.

_____ **4.** Knowing that there was going to be a bakery strike and that in a few days there would not be a loaf on the shelves, he prepared to do his own breadmaking.

_____ **5.** Knowing that tomorrow was a holiday and that all the shops would be closed.

_____ **6.** Because I don't like the new styles and have plenty of clothes I am perfectly happy with.

_____ **7.** To our amazement, the bird flew right into the glass of the closed window.

_____ **8.** As if it didn't make a difference that she had to take two buses and a train to get to school.

_____ **9.** The line at the bank moved slowly.

_____ **10.** Using picks and shovels and working slowly.

The words of a sentence fragment usually belong to the sentence coming just before or just after. You can correct a sentence fragment by joining it to the sentence it is a part of, as in this example:

WRONG: _Walking was difficult. Because wet mud was everywhere and our shoes kept getting stuck._

RIGHT: _Walking was difficult because wet mud was everywhere and our shoes kept getting stuck._

Exercise 11   Five of the following contain a sentence fragment. Revise the sentences to eliminate the fragments. Leave the others alone.

1. They arrived at the party on time. Without, however, the present they had meant to bring.

_____

_____

2. Shouting for help, thrashing wildly about, disappearing in the waves. The swimmer was plainly in trouble.

_____

_____

3. Some people are drawn to supernatural horror. Such creatures as Dracula have a strange fascination for them.

_____

_____

4. Some children leave their toys scattered throughout the house. As though they are marking their day's trail.

_____

_____

5. The price of steak was high. Ground beef, however, was a good buy.

_____

_____

6. Skipping rope is good exercise. It is also less trouble than jogging.

_____

_____

7. Feeling ill, he asked to be excused. Everybody looked at him curiously.

_____

_____

8. Everything would have been all right. If only you had told me that you love me.

_____

_____

9. Counting my change very carefully, not once but twice. I realized that the clerk had given me too much.

_____

_____

10. More and more people are eating fish. Therefore, it has become expensive.

_____

_____

COMPUTER HINT

If you have trouble with sentence fragments, try numbering each of the sentences in your paper. Then, with the use of the return (or enter) key, arrange the sentences as if they make up an exercise like the one above. Then work through the "exercise" item by item, revising as necessary. When you've finished, delete the numbers and the hard returns to put the sentences back in paragraph form.

Avoiding Redundancy

In writing, it is desirable to make every word count, to avoid using unnecessary words. In a first draft, we sometimes are redundant. We unintentionally repeat ourselves by using different words that say the same thing twice. Look at this sentence.

The telephone rang at three a.m. in the morning and woke me up.

Here the same meaning is repeated unnecessarily by *a.m.* and *in the morning*. One or the other should be eliminated.

Look at another example of redundancy:

Please send me the following books listed below.

Here the same meaning is repeated unnecessarily by *following* and *listed below*. One or the other should be eliminated.

Exercise 12 By crossing out unnecessary words, revise each of the following sentences to eliminate the redundancy.

1. With his first arrow, Robin Hood killed the bear dead.
2. In my opinion, I believe that football is causing too many injuries.
3. As a rule, the hero usually triumphs over the villain.
4. In the future that lies ahead, we may travel to distant planets.
5. Using her new food processor, she blended the ingredients together.
6. As a handsome unmarried bachelor, he gets lots of attention from the girls.
7. In modern times, women have assumed new roles today.
8. The choice of our new car was selected by my mother.
9. As far as we know, there is no life on the moon to the best of our knowledge.
10. They didn't return the book back to the library.

Modeling

After you have gone through the exercises, return to the literary models on pages 1–2. Notice how the writers avoid sentence fragments. Pay particular attention to Twain's use of semicolons to join short sentences into series that sweep the reader through the descriptive text. And finally, notice that all three literary selections are tightly written. No evidence of redundancy here!

When you have finished the exercises and studied the models, give your composition a final proofreading.

Peer or Self-Editing Guidelines

Before you prepare a final copy of your description of a weather experience, ask a peer or peers to read it and use the following guidelines for offering suggestions. Or use the guidelines as a means of self-evaluation.

	very well	1	2	3	4	poorly
1. How well does the description incorporate good picture-making words and phrases?						
2. How well does the paper maintain unity?						
3. How well does the writer move the reader along a chain of meaning with the use of transitions?						
4. How well does the description demonstrate the use of complete sentences?						
5. How well does the writer eliminate redundancy?						

The Final Draft: Sharing

Now is the time to prepare your paper for formal sharing. Think of this step as the "publication" step. You have worked carefully. You have revised and proofread. You have asked peers to respond to your work. Now, using your peers' suggestions and/or your self-evaluation, prepare a final draft of your composition. Add a title. Read again to check for final details.

> ### COMPUTER HINT
>
> When you complete your final draft and print your final copy, be sure to save the text on disk. Any minor corrections you wish to make later can thus be completed in minutes, perhaps seconds.
>
> Be sure to save all files for the course: you will be asked to refer to them later.

Unit 2

A Letter About Language

PREWRITING

Reading the Literature

Most writers know the thesaurus as a companion, a friendly keeper of synonyms and antonyms, kinder than a dictionary. The article below, which appeared in *The New York Times* January 18, 1979, celebrates the bicentennial anniversary of *Roget's Thesaurus*. As you read to enjoy Herbert Mitgang's commemorative words, think about how the English language has changed in recent years.

THESAURUS, AT 200, STILL LOOKS FOR (SEEKS) WORDS
by Herbert Mitgang

Today is an anniversary (celebration, commemoration, festivity, ceremony, tribute, salute).

Two hundred years ago, on Jan. 18, Peter Mark Roget, creator of the Thesaurus of synonyms, antonyms, and related words, was born on Broadwick Street, near Soho Square in London. Users of the English language remain grateful to him to this day.

Fortunately, Roget was a prodigy. He entered the University of Edinburgh at 14, graduated at 19 from its medical school and embarked on a career in science and medicine. He designed a pocket chessboard, devised a slide rule, and tried to perfect a calculator. He was also ahead of his time as an environmentalist.

But Roget is best remembered for his Thesaurus, derived from the Greek word for storehouse or treasury. He spent 47 years compiling a catalogue of words, organized by their meanings. It was published in England in 1852. By the time he died at 90 in 1869, the book had gone through 28 editions.

FIRST U.S. EDITION IN 1886

Thomas Y. Crowell, the leading American publisher of the Thesaurus, picked up a set of plates at auction and brought out his first edition in 1886.

The publishing house is still selling hundreds of thousands of copies annually as *Roget's International Thesaurus*.

The difference between Roget's and other word finders, Patrick Barrett, Crowell's reference book editor, says is that the original scheme is retained—arranging words and phrases in clusters by a single thought or concept rather than in an A-to-Z dictionary format. St. Martin's Press also puts out a Roget in this style; it was last revised in 1965 and is called *The Original Roget's Thesaurus of English Words and Phrases*.

What makes the Thesaurus a living book is that its language is constantly brought up to date (abreast of, with-it, au courant).

ARGOT OF THE 60s AND 70s

The 1977 edition, which added synonyms and antonyms from the 60s and 70s, includes such words as the following in these sample fields:

Environment—*recycle* and *biodegradable*.
Politics—*clout, stonewall, bite the bullet, deep-six, jawbone,* and *eyeball-to-eyeball*.
Business—*bottom line* and *bottom out*.
Entertainment—*sitcom, soap, spaghetti Western, groupie, dingbat*.
Food—*junk food, fast food, stir-fry,* and *macrobiotics*.
Transportation—*jet lag* and *skyjacking*.
Intelligence—*blow one's cover* and *dirty tricks*.
Space—*go*.
General slang—*the pits, honcho, boss, bazoom, zilch, shades, bonkers, bananas,* and *the crunch*.

NEW CANDIDATES

Mr. Barrett says the Crowell reference department is now filing away what he calls "candidates" for inclusion in a new edition. Some may fall away from disuse; most will probably stick, such as these words:

Upscale, an advertising derivative for people with money.
Double-dipper, a person on a pension who then goes on salary.
No-frills, stripped to bare essentials as in no meals on a flight.
Kneecapping, shooting in the knees, an Italian terrorist method.
Pop, a transaction or sale, as in "$10 a pop."
Swagging, appropriating government property for personal use.
Push-in's, mugging at the door.
Android, an automaton, a not-quite human fellow.

All of which means that Roget's has a future (hereafter, by-and-by, aftertime, imminent, in the fullness of time, eventually, sooner or later).

Reader Response

"Thesaurus, at 200" pays tribute to Peter Mark Roget and piques reader curiosity about language changes. Perhaps the article triggered the recollection of at least one language-change encounter in which you may have heard or read a new word or expression that caused you pause.

As you think about your reaction to Mitgang's article, consider these questions:

a. How many of the words Mitgang lists as "new" for the 1977 edition are included in the current edition? Which ones?

b. How many of the new candidates made it into the current edition? Which ones?

Brainstorm with two or three classmates to list as many new words as you can, words that should be candidates for the next edition. These could be words or expressions that are used by your friends or schoolmates, or on television or radio, or in newspapers and magazines. As indicated in the article above, these expressions may have originated from general slang, current affairs, sports, music, science, and entertainment. Perhaps an expression you choose will be a "localism," peculiar to your own school, town, or region. To judge the validity of your list, check a current thesaurus and/or dictionary to see that your word or phrase is *not* listed. Share your completed list with other classmates, compiling a composite list.

COMPUTER HINT

Appoint a classmate to enter new terms into the computer, alphabetizing the composite list. Then have copies printed for each member of the class. Retain your copy for later.

When you have studied the composite list, turn to your response journal and write informally about your reactions to the Mitgang article, perhaps exploring one or two reasons why you enjoyed—or did not enjoy—the article. Or perhaps you prefer to discuss why one or two of the words or expressions mentioned have significance or appeal to you.

Active Reading

Skim the literary selection again. Look at Mitgang's sentences. Some follow a similar pattern with the subject first and modifying words, phrases, and clauses coming later in the sentence. Look for sentences that begin in a different way. Put a check mark at the beginning of sentences which you think begin with something other than the subject.

Studying Model Writing Techniques

Modifiers in Sentence Variety

REMEMBER! All sorts of choices are open to you in the kinds of words and sentences you use to express yourself.

Look at the following pairs of sentences. How are they very much alike? How are they different?

    a. The hungry baby began to whimper.
    b. Hungry, the baby began to whimper.

    a. The storm struck suddenly.
    b. Suddenly, the storm struck.

    a. The winds, gathering force, began to rattle windows.
    b. Gathering force, the winds began to rattle windows.

    a. They left the room in tears.
    b. In tears, they left the room.

    a. The family lived as though they were rich although they didn't know where their next dime was coming from.
    b. Although they didn't know where their next dime was coming from, the family lived as though they were rich.

Usually, sentences begin with the subject, with modifying words, phrases, and clauses coming later in the sentence. The example sentences marked *a* are written in that order. However, to give sentences variety and interest, we can sometimes begin sentences with the modifying word, phrase, or clause, as in the *b* sentences.

Exercise 1   Find three sentences in Mitgang's article which follow a pattern similar to the *b* sentences. Write them below.

1. _____

_____

2. _____

_____

3. _____

_____

Exercise 2   Try your hand at this technique. Rewrite each of the following sentences so that it begins with the italicized modifier. (Note that when modifiers are placed at the beginning of the sentence, instead of close to the word they modify within the sentence, they are followed by a comma.)

1. The sailors hauled *desperately* on the ropes.

_____

2. The *smiling* child licked his ice-cream cone contentedly.

_____

_____

18

3. The dog, *waving his tail*, approaches us.

_____

4. The rain fell *with relentless persistence*.

_____

5. We had to cancel our trip *because Dad got sick*.

_____

_____

Exercise 3 Try writing some original sentences that begin with modifiers. In each of the following items, you are given a beginning modifier. Complete each sentence with your own words.

1. Tall and strong, _____

_____

2. Sorrowfully, _____

_____

3. Without hesitation, _____

_____

4. Watching television, _____

_____

5. After breakfast, _____

_____

6. When the party was over, _____

_____

7. If you are going to the drugstore, _____

_____

8. Because the ground was covered with leaves, _____

_____

9. Putting on her raincoat, _____

_____

10. Kind and considerate, _____

_____

With these prewriting activities behind you, you are ready to begin writing a first draft of a response to Mitgang's article.

RESPONSE

Modeling

You studied the Mitgang article for sentence variety, especially how he begins sentences. Notice that while some sentences begin with modifiers, certainly not all do. Readers subconsciously look for that variety to let them hear an inner sense of rhythm in the writing. The change in sentence structure also helps writers achieve emphasis. Exercises 1–3 above helped you work with sentence beginnings.

Turn to your journal in which you wrote a response to the Mitgang article. Even though journal entries are informal and not intended for other readers, study your sentence beginnings. Do some begin with modifiers? Or can you alter some so that they do?

Writing

The following writing assignment will give you the opportunity to follow the model and strive for sentence variety. Although you may choose and develop your own subject, you may wish to consider the following suggestions:

Give your reactions to the article on pages 15–16 in the form of a letter to Robert L. Chapman, the editor of the current edition of the Thesaurus.

You will probably want to begin by noting that you have read the article by Herbert Mitgang in *The New York Times* of January 18, 1979. You may then wish to give one or two general reasons why you found the article enjoyable. As one example, you might point out that the article made you aware that the English language is a rich one, offering the choice of many synonymous words and phrases, each of which has its own unique flavor. As another example, you might mention the fact that the article makes clear that the English language is constantly changing and enriching itself with new words and expressions from various sources, such as general slang, politics, science, and sports.

The aim of your second paragraph may well be to make more specific the general appreciation expressed in the first paragraph. Here you would discuss one, two, or three of the words or expressions mentioned in the article that have particular significance or appeal for you. Perhaps the term *no-frills* recalls and sums up perfectly an experience with physical hardship you have had. Have you had the occasion to *stonewall*, or have you been *in the pits*? Do you know someone who is appropriately described as an *android*? Does *junk food* or *macrobiotics* have application to your life-style? If you are inspired to write extensively about the applicability of two or more words or expressions to your own experience, you may find that you have enough material to justify two paragraphs (a third as well as a second).

You may wish to devote your concluding paragraph to recommending for inclusion in the next edition of the Thesaurus one or more currently popular words or expressions not mentioned in the article. Besides mentioning the words or expressions, you should give their meanings and, if possible, their origins. You might also explain why you feel the word or expression is likely to be enduring and therefore merits a place in the Thesaurus.

In this first draft, concentrate on the subject matter: your ideas and their supporting details. Later, you will revise and polish.

REVISION

Now that you have completed the first draft of your letter about language, you are ready to revise. In the revision process, we will focus on organization, chains of meaning, and proofreading details. Use these materials as a model for your own revision process.

Checking Organization

General and Specific

REMEMBER! Organized thinking is essential in composition writing.

Many writers organize their material from the general to the specific. They begin, as Mitgang does, with broad informative ideas and then move to specific details.

An important skill of organization is the ability to distinguish between the general and the specific and to see relationships between them. The following exercise asks you to respond to Mitgang's article. The next exercise applies the general principles to other content.

Exercise 4 List below fifteen general and fifteen specific words from Herbert Mitgang's article. Do not use words from the argot and candidates lists. Three are completed for you.

GENERAL WORDS/PHRASES		SPECIFIC WORDS/PHRASES
creator	1.	*Peter Mark Roget*
word finders	2.	*Roget's*
scheme	3.	*dictionary format*
_____	4.	_____
_____	5.	_____
_____	6.	_____

7. _____

8. _____

9. _____

10. _____

11. _____

12. _____

13. _____

14. _____

15. _____

Exercise 5   In each of the following groups, circle the one item that includes all the others and could serve as a title or heading for them.

1. humidity, rainfall, temperature, weather, winds

2. books, journals, magazines, newspapers, publications

3. crime, inflation, pollution, problems, unemployment

4. autos, computers, industries, oil, steel

5. cleanliness, exercise, health, nutrition, sleep

6. blues, country, jazz, music, rock

7. baking, broiling, cooking, roasting, simmering

8. face, hands, spring, stem, watch

9. insect, gnat, grasshopper, mosquito, moth

10. czar, emperor, king, ruler, shah

11. bricklayer, carpenter, mechanic, plasterer, worker

12. expression, frown, smile, sneer, stare

13. deed, contract, document, lease, will

14. ability, education, experience, industriousness, qualifications

15. ammeter, gauge, instrument, microscope, scale

Modeling

Review the Mitgang article. Notice that he begins with general background and ideas. As the article progresses, he becomes more and more specific.

Look at your own work in progress. Does your letter of response begin with a general idea which you then support with specific references? Make revisions as necessary.

Checking Chains of Meaning

Functions of Transition Words

REMEMBER! In composition writing, sentences are not individual or isolated. Instead, the thought is carried along from sentence to sentence in a chain of meaning.

Sentences written in sequence are held together by chains of meaning. Those chains take definite forms that can be expressed by transition words and phrases. The following chart lists transition words and phrases grouped according to the specific idea or relationship that each word or phrase expresses. Study the list. Then do the exercises that follow.

RELATIONSHIP EXPRESSED	TRANSITION WORD OR PHRASE
Add another thought or emphasize a thought.	*besides, also, what's more, furthermore, in addition, again*
Arrange ideas in order of time, space, logic, or importance.	*first, next, then, finally, meanwhile, later, afterward, eventually, nearly, above, below, in front, beyond, to the right, to the left*
Connect contrasting or opposite ideas.	*still, however, on the one hand . . . on the other hand, yet, nevertheless, rather, on the contrary*
Add an illustration or explanation to an idea.	*for example, for instance, in other words, specifically*
Show that one idea is a consequence, or result, of another.	*so, therefore, consequently, accordingly*
Show that one idea is an exception to or limitation of another idea.	*of course, though, to be sure*
Show one idea as a summary of another idea.	*in short, in brief, to sum up*
Show a similarity between ideas.	*in the same way, similarly, likewise*

Exercise 6   Find at least eight transition words or phrases from Mitgang's article. Determine the relationship expressed.

TRANSITION WORD/PHRASE	RELATIONSHIP EXPRESSED
fortunately	1. *emphasize a thought*
	2.
	3.
	5.
	5.
	6.
	7.
	8.

Exercise 7 Here is a list of pairs of sentences. From the parentheses following each pair of sentences, choose the transition word or phrase that best expresses the chain of meaning between the two sentences. Write your choice in the blank.

1. Would you like to start collecting stamps? _____, go to the library and take out a beginner's book on the hobby.
   (Consequently, In brief, First)

2. When you are first learning to play any musical instrument, the task seems hopeless. _____, as you continue to practice, you begin to see yourself making steady progress.
   (However, Besides, Accordingly)

3. She is an excellent swimmer. _____, she is a fine all-around athlete.
   (Indeed, Nevertheless, Accordingly)

4. Let the sauce simmer in the pan for at least an hour. You can begin, _____, to prepare the meat.
   (above, on the other hand, meanwhile)

5. Most people didn't like the new styles that the manufacturers were introducing. _____, prices for clothing had simply gotten too high.
   (For example, So, Besides)

6. Professional athletes can have enormous incomes. Nancy Lopez, _____, earned over one hundred thousand dollars in her rookie year as a golf pro.
   (for example, so, besides)

7. Because of carefully planned efforts, we are now waging a successful fight against damage to the environment. _____, we see that we can begin to solve our problems if we have the will.
   (Therefore, Again, Later)

8. Angela was talented in math and science. Her sister, _____, was interested in golf and tennis.
   (to be sure, on the other hand, consequently)

9. Most basketball players are well above six feet tall. _____, there are some notable exceptions.
   (To be sure, In fact, Eventually)

10. The city itself lies in a valley. _____, the mountains can be seen rising majestically.
    (Yet, Below, Beyond)

11. The dangers to health of cigarette smoking have been proved beyond a doubt. _____, people who continue to smoke are deliberately committing slow suicide.
    (Also, In other words, Finally)

12. Conservation measures seem to be the only short-range answer to the energy problem. Such measures, _____, will merely postpone the day of reckoning, the day when there simply is no more oil or coal or gas.
    (Consequently, however, moreover)

13. Some scientists think that items not now usually considered eatable will one day form

an important part of our diet. _____, seaweed will appear on restaurant menus.
(For instance, Besides, In the same way)

14. Improper punctuation can obscure the meaning intended by the writer. _____,
misspellings, such as *then* for *than*, may interfere with communication.
(Specifically, Similarly, Nevertheless)

15. For a long time, we were taught by myth and fairy tale that the wolf was a vicious

animal, an enemy to humans. _____, it is now believed, the wolf is an attractive,
harmless creature, important in nature's scheme.
(On the contrary, Beyond, Similarly)

Modeling

Notice the frequency of transitional words and phrases Mitgang uses to connect ideas and show logical relationships.

Read your own work in progress. Have you included chains of meaning? Ask a peer or peers to check, too. Add any necessary transition words and phrases to help your reader follow your meaning.

Proofreading

The final step in revising is proofreading—checking the grammar, usage, and mechanics details. Look for errors in spelling and punctuation. Then, study the following section for two common errors emphasized for your attention: wordiness and run-on sentences. The exercises that follow will help you recognize and avoid these errors in your writing.

Checking Wordiness

In writing, it is desirable to make every word count, to avoid using unnecessary words. As you learned in Unit 1, we are sometimes redundant in writing a first draft. Redundance is one form of wordiness; there are others. Look at the following examples.

WORDY: *Abraham Lincoln was a person who was humble.*
CONCISE: *Abraham Lincoln was humble.*

WORDY: *It is probable that we shall have a harsh winter.*
CONCISE: *We shall probably have a harsh winter.*

WORDY: *He lives in the vicinity of Pittsfield, Massachusetts.*
CONCISE: *He lives near Pittsfield, Massachusetts.*

WORDY: *That section of the library is reserved for study purposes.*
CONCISE: *That section of the library is reserved for study.*

WORDY: *He stopped the car in an abrupt manner.*
CONCISE: *He stopped the car abruptly.*

WORDY: *We haven't decided the question as to whether we should go by car or train.*
CONCISE: *We haven't decided whether we should go by car or train.*

WORDY: *The goal that I am working for is to lose ten pounds.*
CONCISE: *My goal is to lose ten pounds.*

WORDY: *In spite of the fact that he is lazy, I like him.*
CONCISE: *In spite of his laziness, I like him.*

WORDY: *He always thought he would be successful along scientific lines.*
CONCISE: *He always thought he would be successful in science.*

WORDY: *The snow lay like a blanket. It covered the countryside.*
CONCISE: *The snow blanketed the countryside.*

Exercise 8   Rewrite each of the following sentences to make it concise.

1. The reason that we are meeting is that we need to consider revising the constitution.

2. After a delay of forty-five minutes, the audience got to the point that it became restless and noisy.

3. The crime conditions that existed in the city became intolerable.

4. He glanced at her in a suspicious manner.

5. It is probable that we will have a bumper crop next year.

6. A politician is a person who is quick to promise and slow to act.

7. She seldom discusses any subject that is of a controversial nature.

8. A bird was perched on a branch of the apple tree. The bird was black and orange and it had a sharp beak.

9. Anyone interested in the field of English composition should read this book.

10. His father had an executive-type of position.

_____

_____

11. There are two plays in our anthology, and I like them both.

_____

_____

12. The legislature debated the question as to whether oil prices should be deregulated.

_____

_____

13. There is only one excuse that is acceptable.

_____

_____

14. The door is to be opened for emergency purposes only.

_____

_____

15. Because of the fact that she had been ill, she missed the first two weeks of classes.

_____

_____

Eliminating Run-on Sentences

You know that some groups of words are sentences. You also know that, in our writing system, you begin a sentence with a capital letter and end it with an appropriate end punctuation mark. You know, as well, that in composition writing the thought is continued from sentence to sentence in a chain of meaning.

Sometimes, we wish to show these strong thought connections between two sentences by writing them as one compound sentence. Our writing system allows us to join two sentences as one compound sentence in several ways.

1. We can form a compound sentence by using the conjunction *and*.

SEPARATE SENTENCES: *I dusted the furniture. My brother swept the floor.*
COMPOUND SENTENCE: *I dusted the furniture, and my brother swept the floor.*

2. We can form a compound sentence by using a semicolon (;).

SEPARATE SENTENCES: *I dusted the furniture. My brother swept the floor.*
COMPOUND SENTENCE: *I dusted the furniture; my brother swept the floor.*

3. When appropriate, we can form a compound sentence by using the conjunction *but*.

SEPARATE SENTENCES: *I work slowly. My sister works quickly.*
COMPOUND SENTENCE: *I work slowly, but my sister works quickly.*

Two separate sentences may be joined to form a compound sentence by using a semicolon (;), *and*, or *but*.

Our writing system does **not** permit us to form a compound sentence by using only a comma (,).

> WRONG: *I dusted the furniture, my brother swept the floor.*
> RIGHT: *I dusted the furniture; my brother swept the floor.*
>
> WRONG: *The food was burned, the party was ruined.*
> RIGHT: *The food was burned, and the party was ruined.*
>
> WRONG: *Her car is bigger, mine uses less gas.*
> RIGHT: *Her car is bigger, but mine uses less gas.*

The name usually given to the fairly common error of connecting two sentences with a comma is **run-on sentence.** This error often occurs when the second sentence begins with such words as *then, therefore, however, nevertheless,* and *moreover*. These words are transition adverbs that act as links between sentences. In our writing system they may **not** act to form a compound sentence. When these transition adverbs are used, they must be preceded by either a period or a semicolon.

> WRONG: *I checked the locks on the windows, then I bolted the door.*
> RIGHT: *I checked the locks on the windows. Then I bolted the door.*
> RIGHT: *I checked the locks on the windows; then I bolted the door.*
>
> WRONG: *Organic food is recommended by some people, however, nobody knows just what organic food is.*
> RIGHT: *Organic food is recommended by some people. However, nobody knows just what organic food is.*
> RIGHT: *Organic food is recommended by some people; however, nobody knows just what organic food is.*
>
> WRONG: *The lake appeared to be frozen, nevertheless, we were not sure it was safe to skate on.*
> RIGHT: *The lake appeared to be frozen. Nevertheless, we were not sure it was safe to skate on.*
> RIGHT: *The lake appeared to be frozen; nevertheless, we were not sure it was safe to skate on.*

Exercise 9   Three of the following are correct compound sentences. The remainder are run-on sentences. Do nothing with the correct sentences. Revise the run-on sentences either to separate sentences or to compound sentences.

1. The truck went into a skid, the driver lost control.

_____

_____

2. Shoelaces always break when one is in a hurry; therefore, it is wise to have a spare pair on hand at all times.

_____

_____

3. The tax revolt is widespread in suburban areas, moreover, it is beginning to spread into the cities.

_____

_____

4. The dentist injected Novocain, then he began to drill.

_____

_____

5. The abandoned dogs traveled in packs, they hunted like wolves.

_____

_____

6. The water tasted horrible, but the Health Department claimed it was safe.

_____

_____

7. The park was lovely in spring, cherry blossoms filled the air with their fragrance.

_____

_____

8. We got on the shortest line, however, it turned out to be the slowest.

_____

_____

9. The plane gathered speed, it was in the air before we knew it.

_____

_____

10. It had rained for three days, and the rivers were rising dangerously.

_____

_____

Modeling

After you have gone through the exercises, return to the model literary selection. Notice how tightly written the Mitgang article is, how he avoids wordiness. And notice, too, that in spite of some rather lengthy sentences, he uses accurate punctuation to avoid run-on sentences. Consider:

a. Two hundred years ago, on Jan. 18, Peter Mark Roget, creator of the Thesaurus of synonyms, antonyms and related words, was born on Broadwick Street, near Soho Square in London.

b. He entered the University of Edinburgh at 14, graduated at 19 from its medical school and embarked on a career in science and medicine.

c. He designed a pocket chessboard, devised a slide rule, and tried to perfect a calculator.

Notice that model sentence *a*, although lengthy, has only a single subject, *Peter Mark Roget*, and a single verb, *was born*. Sentences *b* and *c* both include three-part predicates but only one subject.

When you have finished studying the exercises and the literary model, give your composition a final proofreading.

COMPUTER HINT

If you have trouble with run-on sentences, use the return or enter key to arrange your text as if it were a list of sentences as in exercise 9. Then read each word group to determine if you have a good sentence or a run-on sentence. Correct any errors.

Peer or Self-Editing Guidelines

Before you prepare a final copy of your letter about language, ask a peer or peers to read it and use the following guidelines for offering suggestions. Or use the guidelines as a means of self-evaluation.

	very well	*1*	*2*	*3*	*4*	*poorly*
1. How well does the letter incorporate general and specific words and phrases?						
2. How well does the writer use transition words and phrases?						
3. How well does the writer vary the beginnings of sentences, using modifying words, phrases, and clauses?						
4. How well has the writer eliminated wordiness?						
5. How well has the writer eliminated run-on sentences?						

The Final Draft: Sharing

As you prepare your final draft for the publication stage, take into consideration your peers' suggestions and/or your self-evaluation based on the guidelines above. Add a title. Or, if you wish to maintain the letter format, begin with "Dear Mr. Mitgang." Read again to check for final details.

A Personal
Essay on Friendship

PREWRITING

Reading the Literature

Friendships. How we value them! But sometimes our "friends" disappoint us, leaving us distressed, miserable, maybe even angry. Interpersonal relationships seem to consume big hunks of our time and energy, and psychologists study how those interpersonal relationships affect us. The following article, from *Psychology Today*, talks about what "friendship" means. As you read to enjoy, see how your own definition and experiences fit with those given here.

FRIENDSHIP: AN INQUIRY

We talk about friends a lot. "My friend and I saw a terrific movie last night...." "A friend gave me the name of a good lawyer...." "I was really down, and my friend..." We may use the word *friend* in conversation to refer to someone we've known since grade school, to a person we've worked with for six months, or to someone we'd turn to in a crisis. A friend may be someone whom we see at least twice a week or, at most, once a year; someone who likes the same movies, or maybe someone who doesn't.

If pressed for a definition, we might make a distinction between friends and acquaintances, and, within the category of friends, between close friends and casual friends, and between work friends and neighbors who are friends. Not everyone, however, makes the same distinctions in the same way. Indeed, surprising differences in people's conceptions of friendship emerge when they begin to talk about what it means to them. Just as the philosopher Ludwig Wittgenstein has argued that no single set of characteristics completely defines a "game," it is probably not possible to define a friend in any simple way.

Regardless of whether we can say precisely what the words mean, everyone recognizes the importance of friends and friendship. Poets, novelists, and philosophers have written about the joys, and sometimes the costs, of friendship. And while we who are not poets, novelists, or philosophers may agree or disagree with what they say, we know they are right about the significance of friends.

In fact, friendship seems to be on many people's minds right now: simply mentioning the subject usually provokes an intense and thoughtful conversation—even among people who barely know one another. This interest may reflect an awareness that our conception of friendship—what it is, what we expect from it, what we are willing to give to it—is changing, in a highly mobile society in which values and institutions (particularly the family) are undergoing rapid transformations.

Reader Response

After reading this brief article about friendship, develop a response journal entry in which you respond to the questions below. Remember that a journal entry is informal, is written for your own use, and serves to help you recognize your thoughts. Write freely, as if you were talking to yourself, as you answer these questions:

a. What is your definition of a friend?

b. How do you think a "best friend" differs from other friends?

c. Do you think friends tend to be more like each other or different from each other? Why?

d. Of the friendships you have had, which has meant the most to you? Why?

> ### COMPUTER HINT
> If you work easily with a computer, complete your journal entry at the keyboard. Allow your thoughts to flow without worrying about typing errors, sentence structure, punctuation, or any other mechanical details. Print a copy for your folder and save the prewriting activity under a file name like "journal.fri."

Active Reading

Your word choice determines the message readers get from your writing. To refer to a friend as "nice" gives a different shade of meaning than "congenial," "proper," "respectable," or "amicable"—all synonyms of "nice." Reread the friendship article. Notice the author's words. Underline five words that you think are especially effective in coloring the meaning. Be prepared to explain why you think these words are effective.

Studying Model Writing Techniques

Synonyms and Near-Synonyms

REMEMBER! All sorts of choices are open to you in the kinds of words and sentences you use to express yourself.

The English language is rich in words. For each meaning you may want to express, you can select from among many synonyms and near-synonyms the one word that expresses your meaning most precisely and has exactly the right feeling for the sentence you are writing. The following exercises will help you develop your word-choice skills.

Exercise 1   The following words are from the literary selection about friendship. Use the dictionary or thesaurus to find at least three synonyms or near-synonyms for each of them. Then reread the passage with any of the synonyms or near-synonyms. Does the meaning change in any way?

> Regardless of whether we can *say* precisely what the words *mean*, everyone *recognizes* the *importance* of friends and friendship. Poets, novelists, and philosophers have written about the *joys*, and sometimes the *costs*, of friendship. And while we who are not poets, novelists, or philosophers may *agree or disagree* with what they say, we *know* they are *right* about the *significance* of friends.

SYNONYMS

---

1. say   _____   _____   _____

2. mean   _____   _____   _____

3. recognizes   _____   _____   _____

4. importance   _____   _____   _____

5. joys   _____   _____   _____

6. costs   _____   _____   _____

7. agree or disagree   _____   _____   _____

8. know   _____   _____   _____

9. right   _____   _____   _____

10. significance   _____   _____   _____

Exercise 2   How many synonyms and near-synonyms would you guess there are for the common word *said*? There are many dozens! In the following exercise, each group of ten synonyms for *said* is followed by three short passages in which the word *said* is used. For each passage, decide which synonym of the ten listed is most appropriate in meaning and feeling. Cross out the word *said*, and substitute your own choice from the list.

I

accused	apologized	asserted
advised	argued	bargained
affirmed	asked	barked
answered		

1. "With your aptitudes, you should think of a career in law," the counselor *said*. _____

2. "Straighten up that line!" *said* the top sergeant. _____

3. "Throw in radial tires, and it's a deal," the customer *said*. _____

II

begged	breathed	coaxed
beseeched	chattered	commanded
blurted	claimed	complained
boasted		

4. "Don't answer the bell, and don't make a sound," she *said*. "It's that neighbor wanting to borrow something, and I don't want him to know we're home." _____

5. The child *said*, "Jimmy told me not to tell you he tore his new sweater." _____

6. "Eat all your egg," *said* the father, "and Daddy will buy you a new toy." _____

III

jeered	mentioned	murmured
jested	moaned	narrated
laughed	mocked	objected
lied		

7. "The pain in my leg is terrible, Dr. Welby," *said* the patient. _____

8. Andy *said*, "I suppose you're going to tell us you dropped the ball because the sun was in your eyes." _____

9. "There's a special on canned soup today, Mrs. Rodriguez," the grocer *said*. _____

IV

stuttered	urged	whispered
summarized	warned	wondered
threatened	whimpered	yelled
thundered		

10. "Should I go to the movies or study for the test?" Tom *said*. _____

11. "If we don't cut down on our consumption of energy," *said* the scientist, "the shortage will become disastrous." _____

12. "Please don't make me go to bed," *said* the child. "I never get a chance to watch my TV programs anymore." _____

Exercise 3 Now try using the best word choice in some writing of your own. Below are ten more synonyms for *said*. Choose any three. Write each of the three in an original sentence in which it fits precisely. Underline the synonym for *said* in each sentence.

screamed	snarled	stammered
sermonized	sneered	suggested
sighed	specified	squawked
snapped		

1. _____

_____

2. _____

_____

3. _____

_____

Exercise 4 Here are twenty groups of synonyms and near-synonyms. Study each group, and notice the differences in shades of meaning and feeling among the words. Then choose one word from each group. Compose a sentence in which the exact meaning and feeling of the word fit the meaning and feeling of the sentence. (You may use any form of the word you have chosen.) The first one has been done for you as an example.

1. dog canine mutt puppy

A homeless, starved-looking mutt followed me down the street.

2. see behold spot discern

_____

_____

3. bad evil vicious malevolent

_____

_____

4. task chore labor employment

_____

_____

5. money cash funds lucre

_____

_____

6. walk stride stagger meander

_____

_____

7. elderly   senile   venerable   decrepit

_____

_____

8. argument   quarrel   spat   brawl

_____

_____

9. blaze   glow   glisten   flicker

_____

_____

10. frighten   scare   terrify   alarm

_____

_____

11. large   enormous   big   gross

_____

_____

12. give   donate   award   confer

_____

_____

13. run   scurry   hasten   fly

_____

_____

14. slim   skinny   slender   bony

_____

_____

15. mob   crowd   gathering   assemblage

_____

_____

16. cunning   deceitful   crafty   sly

_____

_____

17. sick   ailing   diseased   infirm

_____

_____

18. intelligent   bright   shrewd   canny

_____

_____

19. lie   tale   falsehood   prevarication

_____

_____

20. ugly   homely   unsightly   repulsive

_____

_____

RESPONSE

Modeling

Think about the importance of word choice illustrated in both the literary selection and the exercises you have done. In this writing assignment, you are going to deal with the complex subject of friends and friendship by writing about your own experiences. You will be writing three or four paragraphs about a specific friend and what the friendship means to you.

Turn to your response journal entry about friendship. Consider your choice of words. Check a dictionary or thesaurus for alternative words which may more precisely convey your meaning. Make changes in your journal to reflect the most precise word choice.

Writing

After studying your journal entry, begin your first draft of a personal essay on friendship. Write about a specific friend and what the friendship means to you. Although you may choose and develop your own subject, consider these suggestions:

In this assignment, you are going to deal with the complex subject of friends and friendship by writing about your own experiences. You will be writing three or four paragraphs about a specific friend and what the friendship means to you.

You may wish to develop your first paragraph by identifying and describing your friend. You can give the name, age, and sex of your friend and some details of the friend's physical appearance. It may be best to plunge right into the specifics in your first sentence: "Nicholas Donisi is a sixteen-year-old young man of average height, shy manner, and gentle voice." In this paragraph, give other relevant facts about your friend, such as occupations, interests, hobbies, and talents.

Your second paragraph can be devoted to the origin and development of the friendship. When, where, how, and why did the friendship begin? Why did it continue?

Your third paragraph can deal with the shape the friendship now takes. What things do you do together? What do you talk about? How often and in what forms do you communicate—in person, by letter, by phone? What plans for the future do you share?

In a fourth and final paragraph, you may wish to discuss your personal feelings about the friendship. Just how important is it to you? Why? You may wish to conclude this paragraph by giving in a sentence or two your own general definition of _friend_ or _friendship_.

As you develop your first draft, concentrate on subject matter: your main ideas and their supporting details. You will revise and polish later.

> ### COMPUTER HINT
>
> You may wish to insert material directly from your journal entry into your first draft. To do so, retrieve the file and use the block command to move the text. If your equipment will allow, retrieve the journal as a separate document (and, therefore, on a separate screen) without merging it into the draft document. That capability will eliminate the need to erase unused journal portions from the draft.

REVISION

Now that you have completed your first draft, you are ready to revise. In the revision process, we will focus on organization, chains of meaning, and proofreading details. Use the materials as a model for your own revision process.

Checking Organization

Classifying

REMEMBER! Organized thinking is essential in composition writing.

An important skill of organization is the ability to classify ideas and things. Classification means seeing which ideas and things go together as a group and why they do so. For instance, the "Friendship" article acknowledges some ways by which friendships can be classified: by length (a year, ten years), by closeness (casual acquaintance, close friend), by proximity (at work, in the neighborhood). The following exercise will give you some practice in the skill of classifying.

Exercise 5 Identify below how friends are classified in the literary selection from *Psychology Today*.

1. In the first paragraph, friends are classified by _____.

2. In the second paragraph, they are classified by _____.

3. In the third paragraph, they are classified by _____.

4. In the last paragraph, they are classified by _____.

Exercise 6 Each of the following groups of six items can be logically divided into two subgroups of three items each. In the spaces provided, divide the items into the two subgroups. Then supply an appropriate subheading for each group, and a title or main heading that includes both subgroups. The first one has been done completely for you as an example. In item 2, the title or main heading and the subheadings are done for you as additional examples.

1. ITEMS: beef carrots pork potatoes spinach veal

MAIN HEADING _____*Foods*_____

SUBHEADING *Meats*_____   SUBHEADING *Vegetables*_____

a. ___*beef*___   a. ___*carrots*___

b. ___*pork*___   b. ___*potatoes*___

c. ___*veal*___   c. ___*spinach*___

2. ITEMS: coal gas sun wind water oil

MAIN HEADING _____*Energy Sources*_____

SUBHEADING *Polluting Sources*_____   SUBHEADING *Clean Sources*_____

a. _____   a. _____

b. _____   b. _____

c. _____   c. _____

3. ITEMS: cows deer goats lions sheep wolves

MAIN HEADING _____

SUBHEADING _____   SUBHEADING _____

a. _____   a. _____

b. _____   b. _____

c. _____   c. _____

4. ITEMS: biology chemistry literature music painting physics

MAIN HEADING _____

SUBHEADING _____   SUBHEADING _____

a. _____   a. _____

b. _____   b. _____

c. _____   c. _____

5. ITEMS: arthritis aspirin heating pad massage rheumatism sprain

MAIN HEADING _____

SUBHEADING _____   SUBHEADING _____

a. _____   a. _____

b. _____   b. _____

c. _____   c. _____

6. ITEMS: cars   computers   corn   cotton   television sets   wheat

MAIN HEADING _____

SUBHEADING _____   SUBHEADING _____

a. _____   a. _____

b. _____   b. _____

c. _____   c. _____

7. ITEMS: bonnet   boots   helmet   shoes   slippers   turban

MAIN HEADING _____

SUBHEADING _____   SUBHEADING _____

a. _____   a. _____

b. _____   b. _____

c. _____   c. _____

8. ITEMS: earthquake   flood   inflation   tornado   unemployment   war

MAIN HEADING _____

SUBHEADING _____   SUBHEADING _____

a. _____   a. _____

b. _____   b. _____

c. _____   c. _____

9. ITEMS: baseball   football   golf   skiing   swimming   soccer

MAIN HEADING _____

SUBHEADING _____   SUBHEADING _____

a. _____   a. _____

b. _____   b. _____

c. _____   c. _____

10. ITEMS: cotton   nylon   orlon   polyester   silk   wool

MAIN HEADING _____

SUBHEADING _____   SUBHEADING _____

a. _____   a. _____

b. _____   b. _____

c. _____   c. _____

11. ITEMS: alcohol cigarettes exercise good nutrition drug abuse rest

MAIN HEADING _____

SUBHEADING _____   SUBHEADING _____

a. _____   a. _____

b. _____   b. _____

c. _____   c. _____

12. ITEMS: anger fear hope joy love sorrow

MAIN HEADING _____

SUBHEADING _____   SUBHEADING _____

a. _____   a. _____

b. _____   b. _____

c. _____   c. _____

13. ITEMS: documentaries movie reruns news broadcasts talk shows
situation comedies soaps

MAIN HEADING _____

SUBHEADING _____   SUBHEADING _____

a. _____   a. _____

b. _____   b. _____

c. _____   c. _____

14. ITEMS: inflation productivity public works programs wage-price controls
unemployment urban decay

MAIN HEADING _____

SUBHEADING _____   SUBHEADING _____

a. _____   a. _____

b. _____   b. _____

c. _____   c. _____

15. ITEMS: appendix bibliography foreword index preface table of contents

MAIN HEADING _____

SUBHEADING _____   SUBHEADING _____

a. _____   a. _____

b. _____   b. _____

c. _____   c. _____

Modeling

The literary selection at the beginning of this unit includes a variety of means for classifying friendship. The author uses classification to help define a particularly elusive term.

Look at your own work in progress. Will classification help you organize all or part of your essay? Ask a peer editor for his or her response. Revise as necessary.

Checking Chains of Meaning

Repetition and Pronouns

REMEMBER! In composition writing, sentences are not individual or isolated. Instead, the thought is carried along from sentence to sentence in a chain of meaning.

You have studied how transition words and phrases help tie together ideas in writing. Another device for coherence is **repetition.** Key words and phrases in a sentence may be repeated, or other words may be used to refer to the same idea. **Pronouns,** too, serve as devices for coherence by referring to persons or ideas mentioned in preceding sentences.

For example, look for repeated words, ideas, and pronouns in the following passage:

> The mound-building ants remove every blade of grass and every twig from the clean-swept dooryards. These cleared areas provide a number of benefits for the colonies. In the first place, they are like the clearings of the pioneers; enemies are in the open when they approach the nest. Again, and more important, the bare area retains less moisture than ground covered with vegetation. Moreover, if the ground were not cleared, the roots of plants growing close to the nests would penetrate them and provide channels for water to enter the galleries and caverns.

Now read the passage and note the explanations. The use of transition words and phrases, repetition, and pronouns is identified in parentheses.

> The mound-building ants remove every blade of grass and every twig from the clean-swept dooryards. *These cleared areas* (repeats the meaning of *clean-swept dooryards*) provide a number of benefits for the *colonies* (repeats the meaning of *mound*). *In the first place* (transition phrase), *they* (refers to *cleared areas*) are like the clearings of the pioneers; enemies are in the open when they approach the *nest* (repeats the meaning of *mound-building ants* and *colonies*). *Again*, and *more important* (transition phrases), the *bare area* (repeats the meaning of *clean-swept dooryards* and *cleared areas*) retains less moisture than ground covered with vegetation. *Moreover* (transition word), if the ground were not cleared, the roots of *plants growing close* (repeats the meaning of *ground covered with vegetation*) to the *nests* (repeats *nests*) would penetrate *them* (refers to *nests*) and provide channels for water to enter the *galleries and caverns* (repeats the meaning of *mound, colonies, nests*).

Exercise 7 Review the literary selection on friendship. Underline the transitions which are pronouns or which repeat key words or phrases.

Exercise 8 Read the following passage. In the spaces provided, list at least one example of a transition word or phrase found in the passage. Then list at least one example of words that repeat meanings. If you can find more examples, list them. Circle all of the pronouns used in the passage that refer to previously used nouns. Draw an arrow from each such pronoun to the word it refers to.

> There were times later on when our trail swung away from the river, and the sound of its running water was inaudible. Then the stillness of the forest became intense. In such a silence, we rested once beside a mossy tree stump. Down the trail a falling leaf descended from the lower branch of an Oregon maple. It rode the air in a wide spiral, sliding to a stop like a landing airplane. Although it was fully one hundred feet away, in that profound silence our ears caught the scraping of its stem along the ground.

1. Transition words

_____

2. Words that repeat meanings

_____

_____

_____

Exercise 9 Now try writing original sentence sequences. Use transition words and phrases, words that repeat meanings, and pronouns to help ensure coherence.

In each item below, you are given the first few words of the first sentence. Complete that sentence, and then create a sentence sequence by adding two more sentences.

1. On reaching the age of _____

_____

_____

2. The circus _____

_____

_____

3. My friend _____

_____

_____

4. The last _____

_____

_____

5. After dark _____

_____

_____

Modeling

Read your own work in progress. Have you included transitions to connect ideas for your readers? Ask a peer editor to underline examples of transitional pronouns or repeated key words or phrases. If he or she finds none, consider revising to add chains of meaning for your readers.

Proofreading

The final step in revising is proofreading—checking the grammar, usage, and mechanics details. Two common errors are emphasized for your attention: subject-verb agreement and the use of commas. The exercises that follow will help you to recognize and avoid these errors in your writing.

Subject-Verb Agreement

The core of all sentences is the subject-verb relationship. The subject and verb must work together as closely as the two opposite poles on a magnet.

If the subject is singular in number, the verb must be singular in number.

SINGULAR: An elephant eats a lot.
Orlon is a synthetic fabric.
The train has been late every day.

If the subject is plural in number, the verb must be plural in number.

PLURAL: Elephants eat a lot.
Orlon and nylon are synthetic fabrics.
The trains have been late every day.

In most cases, you will have little trouble in your writing with agreement between subject and verb.

Exercise 10 Five of the following sentences are correct. In the other five, the subject and verb do not agree in number. In these sentences, cross out the incorrect verb and rewrite it so that it agrees with the subject in number.

1. Greyhounds run fast. _____

2. That actor mumbles his lines. _____

3. Two sweaters is hanging in the closet. _____

4. The girls has organized a softball team. _____

5. Are she your best friend? _____

6. Wood and oil are natural fuels. _____

7. The train stop at this station at noon every day. _____

8. Senior citizens live in this project. _____

9. Which dresses are too expensive? _____

10. The clouds is gathering. _____

No doubt you found that exercise easy. However, some sentences present harder problems and require special attention. Look at the following cases.

1. In some sentences, a singular subject is followed by a prepositional phrase containing a plural noun that falls next to the verb. The verb must agree with the singular subject.

    RIGHT: A *swarm* of bees *is coming* toward us.
    WRONG: A swarm of bees are coming toward us.

    RIGHT: *One* of the musicians *plays* a solo.
    WRONG: One of the musicians play a solo.

2. In some sentences, a plural subject is followed by a prepositional phrase containing a singular noun that falls next to the verb. The verb must agree with the plural subject.

    RIGHT: *The* results *of the new system* are *already noticeable.*
    WRONG: *The results of the new system is already noticeable.*

    RIGHT: *The* costs *of constructing one satellite* are *astronomical.*
    WRONG: *The costs of constructing one satellite is astronomical.*

3. The word *and* is used to connect two singular subjects to form a compound subject calling for a plural verb. However, such phrases as *along with*, *together with*, and *as well as* do **not** act to form a compound subject. If the subject preceding these phrases is singular, then the verb must be singular.

    RIGHT: *The* horse, *along with its rider,* was *ready for the race.*
    WRONG: *The* horse, *along with its rider,* were *ready for the race.*

    RIGHT: *The* teacher, *together with his students,* looks *forward to graduation.*
    WRONG: *The* teacher, *together with his students,* look *forward to graduation.*

    RIGHT: Frank, *as well as Frances,* is going *to the dance.*
    WRONG: *Frank, as well as Frances, are going to the dance.*

4. The words *or, either . . . or,* and *neither . . . nor* do not act to form a compound subject. When these connectives are used, the verb agrees in number with the part of the subject that is closer to the verb.

    RIGHT: *Potatoes or* spaghetti *is not as fattening as beef.*
    WRONG: *Potatoes or spaghetti are not as fattening as beef.*

    RIGHT: *Either the blue* shirt *or the yellow* one *is a good match for the tie.*
    WRONG: *Either the blue shirt or the yellow one are a good match for the tie.*

RIGHT:	*Neither Marie nor her sisters are going to the beach.*
WRONG:	*Neither Marie nor her sisters is going to the beach.*

5. In sentences introduced by the word *there*, the subject comes after the verb. The word *there* is not the subject. The verb must agree with the true subject in number.

RIGHT:	*There are a dozen eggs in the refrigerator.*
WRONG:	*There is a dozen eggs in the refrigerator.*
WRONG:	*There's a dozen eggs in the refrigerator.*

6. In a question, the true subject comes after all or part of the verb. The interrogative word that begins the question is never the subject of the sentence.

RIGHT:	*Where are the others?*
WRONG:	*Where is the others?*
WRONG:	*Where's the others?*

RIGHT:	*Have the guests left?*
WRONG:	*Has the guests left?*

Exercise 11   Decide whether the subject in each sentence is singular or plural. Then cross out the incorrect form of the verb given in parentheses.

1. There (*is, are*) two runners on base.

2. Strawberries or ice cream (*is, are*) the choice for dessert.

3. The seal along with the dolphin (*needs, need*) to breathe air.

4. A half pint of blueberries now (*costs, cost*) more than ten pounds of potatoes.

5. Where (*do, does*) blueberries come from?

6. Neither the players nor the coach (*expects, expect*) to win the last game.

7. A pair of jogging shoes as well as a track suit and sweatband (*was, were*) found in the empty locker.

8. Golf alone among all sports (*requires, require*) the striking of a stationary ball.

9. Cabbage, together with carrot and onion, (*was, were*) thrown into the pot.

10. A formation of wild geese (*knifes, knife*) across the sky.

Uses of the Comma

In our writing system, the comma helps to clarify and sometimes drastically change meaning, as the following pairs of sentences illustrate.

Please let me have some honey.
Please let me have some, honey.

Bob, the dog is barking.
Bob, the dog, is barking.

Polluting my friends is not acceptable.
Polluting, my friends, is not acceptable.

Exercise 12 Each of the following sentences will cause a reader trouble unless a comma is inserted to tell the reader where to pause. Insert the comma in the appropriate place.

1. While we were eating the dog began to bark.

2. Two years before the peace treaty had been signed.

3. As I was leaving my wife returned.

4. On the path leading to the cellar steps were heard.

5. I don't see anyone but my sister is sure someone is hiding in the woods.

Of the various uses of commas, there are two uses in which errors are commonly made. We will concentrate on these two common errors in the use of commas.

A comma is often required to separate introductory words, phrases, and clauses from the main part of the sentence. This use of the comma is illustrated by sentences 1 to 4 in Exercise 12, and by the following examples:

> In other words, crash diets are a poor way to lose weight.
> Later, we defrosted the refrigerator and rearranged the closets.
> Straining at the pedals with all her strength, the cyclist made it up the steep hill.
> Because the fire fighters were well trained and efficient, they prevented a major disaster.

Exercise 13 Place a comma in each of the following sentences to separate introductory words, phrases, and clauses from the rest of the sentence.

1. Although he has never shown any mechanical skill he wants to be an engineer.

2. Refreshed by the long rest the explorers once again took to the trail.

3. Finally the fat should be drained off.

4. For example many lawyers had no formal education in those days.

5. While the baby is napping you must be quiet.

6. Disappointed with the performance of the mayor the voters supported her opponent.

7. Above all other things I value the company of a good friend.

8. On the other hand the trip was very expensive.

9. If we change to the metric system many people will find the adjustment difficult.

10. In a long envelope with a strange postmark they found a check for a thousand dollars.

Sometimes words that interrupt the main thought occur in the middle of a sentence. Such words must be separated from the rest of the sentence by *two* commas. To use only one comma in such cases is worse than using none at all, for then the comma illogically breaks the sentence in half.

Words and phrases in apposition, words and phrases of direct address, and parenthetical remarks must be separated by *two* commas when they occur in the middle of a sentence.

Apposition

WRONG: *The United States a nation of 250 million people has been blessed with rich natural resources.*

WRONG: *The United States a nation of 250 million people, has been blessed with rich natural resources.*

RIGHT: *The United States, a nation of 250 million people, has been blessed with rich natural resources.*

Direct Address

WRONG: *What can we do fellow sufferers about those endless and tiresome commercials?*

WRONG: *What can we do, fellow sufferers about those endless and tiresome commercials?*

RIGHT: *What can we do, fellow sufferers, about those endless and tiresome commercials?*

Parenthetical Remarks

WRONG: *India in my opinion will one day be a great world power.*

WRONG: *India, in my opinion will one day be a great world power.*

RIGHT: *India, in my opinion, will one day be a great world power.*

Exercise 14   Insert the missing comma in each of the following sentences.

1. Los Angeles to repeat what I have said before, is unlike any other large city.

2. The German shepherd, a beautiful animal is an affectionate pet.

3. We are going to give up my friend, before we go any farther.

4. The meat, as far as I am concerned is overcooked.

5. The damage we can be sure, will be repaired.

6. He walked, a free man through the prison gates.

7. The decision, fellow students cannot be postponed.

8. The parents not the children, are at fault.

9. Many sources newspapers as well as books, can be used in your research.

10. It is time my child, for you to give up sucking your thumb.

Modeling

After you have gone through the exercises, return to the literary model. Notice the subject-verb relationships. Can you find them? Then check the use of commas. See if you can spot the rule for commas included in the essay. Consider:

a. If pressed for a definition, we might make a distinction between friends and acquaintances. . . . (to set apart an introductory phrase)

b. Indeed, surprising differences in people's conceptions of friendship emerge. . . . (to set apart an introductory word)

c. Not everyone, however, makes the same distinctions in the same way. (to set off a parenthetical word)

d. . . . and, within the category of friends, between close friends and casual friends . . . (to set off a parenthetical phrase)

Note, too, how the punctuation helps readers follow the writer's thoughts. For instance, commas separate items in a series in these model sentences:

    e. We may use the word *friend* in a conversation to refer to someone we've known since grade school, to a person we've worked with for six months, or to someone we'd turn to in a crisis.

    f. This interest may reflect an awareness that our conception of friendship—what it is, what we expect from it, what we are willing to give to it—is changing. . . .

When you have completed the exercises and studied the model, give your composition a final proofreading.

Peer or Self-Editing Guidelines

Before you prepare a final copy of your personal essay on friendship, ask a peer or peers to read it and use the following guidelines for offering suggestions. Or use the guidelines as a means of self-evaluation.

	very well	*1*	*2*	*3*	*4*	*poorly*
1. How well does the composition demonstrate shades of meaning by the accurate use of synonyms and near-synonyms?						
2. How well does the writer use repetition and pronouns to create chains of meaning?						
3. How well does the composition display techniques of classification?						
4. How well has the writer made subjects agree with their verbs?						
5. How well has the writer used commas?						

The Final Draft: Sharing

As you prepare your final draft for the publication stage, take into consideration your peers' suggestions and/or your self-evaluation based on the guidelines. Add a title. Then read again to check for final details.

Unit 4

A Narrative About a Foolish Action or Decision

PREWRITING

Reading the Literature

At one time or another, everyone is led to do something foolish that results, at the least, in embarrassment and, at the most, in some kind of severe personal loss. The following story by Don James recounts one such decision and subsequent results. As you read to enjoy the following literary selection, try to identify with Danny or Ricco. Think about some foolish decision or action that you or someone you know carried out.

CHICKEN! by Don James

Four boys were lounging against the side of Danny's car at the drive-in, and their girls were sitting inside. The male talk was about cars.

Suddenly Ricco, a slim, dark-complexioned boy, smiled thinly at Danny. "You still chicken to drag?" he asked.

Danny smiled, but there was a little nervousness in the smile. "I'm not chicken," he said. "I can take you in that car of yours anytime. So why bother?"

"Big talk," Ricco said, still smiling. The kids felt a tenseness in the air, and the girls stopped talking. Everyone was watching the two boys. "Chicken?" Ricco asked again, a sharp challenge in his voice.

"No," Danny said quietly. "I'm not chicken."

"OK? How's about it?"

For a second Danny hesitated. He glanced at Florence, his girl, and she suddenly appeared to be frightened. She shook her head a little. Danny shrugged his shoulders and managed a tight grin.

"It's on," he nodded. "Mill Highway?"

A twenty-mile stretch of highway to a mill was a favorite for drag racing. It had light traffic, with only occasional trucks going to and from the mill. At night the highway was deserted, and seldom did a state patrol car drive it.

It included a straight stretch, curves, hills, and a hair-raising half mile along the edge of a hundred-foot-deep canyon. The highway was so located that a car at the far end of the racing strip, on top of a hill, could be seen from the starting point. A lookout from there could see almost ten miles down a straightaway toward the mill. When the highway was clear, he could signal for the start by flashing his headlights toward the waiting racers.

"Don't do it. Danny," Florence was almost crying. "Please. He's dirty. You know he is. It's not that you aren't a better driver—it's just that . . . well, you can't trust him. Danny, I'm afraid."

"It's OK," he told her. "I'm not afraid. I can take him."

"But Danny—"

"Look, Flo—I can't be chicken, can I?"

"You're not chicken. Everyone knows that! Ricco's just trying to—"

"Forget it, honey. He's needled me once too often. Somebody's ripe to take him."

Florence looked up at him, started to say something, and then closed her lips tightly when she saw the expression on his face. She tried not to let the tears come to her eyes, and she stood on her toes and kissed him before she turned and hurried to the carload of youngsters waiting for her.

Twenty minutes later Danny and Ricco waited side by side in their cars, engines running, eyes glued to a far hilltop where the lookout car was stationed.

A light flashed twice on the hilltop—the signal. They were doing well over a hundred miles an hour when they went into the first curve, side by side. Danny was on the inside. He let up on the gas before hitting the curve, and then hit the gas pedal when he was into the curve to whip the car around. Ricco was using the same racing tactics.

They roared down a long, straight descent for a mile, gunning their cars for the first climbing grade. They were still even as they topped the rise, and now Ricco edged close to Danny.

Danny recognized the maneuver. He narrowed his eyes, held his wheel steady, and jammed the gas pedal to the floorboard. Ricco was not going to force him off the highway or to fall back. He wasn't chicken. Ricco pulled away.

Both drivers clamped hard on the gas again. The speedometer needles climbed—105, 108, 109 . . . Danny felt the steering wheel grow slick under the sweat of his hands. He hunched over. Faster—faster—the roar of the car engines, the wail of wind around the windshield—faster—faster.

They tore into a downgrade and were on the canyon rim. Ricco was next to the drop. Slowly he began to edge toward Danny—just inches—a steady, speed-mad pressure. Danny set his mouth. There was a soft shoulder off the blacktop on his side. He couldn't give more.

Ricco edged again. The fenders touched and the cars bounced apart. Danny felt his car sway, and he fought the wheel. He saw Ricco sway toward him and the cars touched again, and this time Danny felt the car careen wildly as he fought the wheel to hold his place on the highway.

From the corner of his eye, he saw Ricco's headlights cast a light toward the far side of the canyon, and a few seconds later he dimly heard a faraway crash. Ricco no longer was beside him, and he was strangely alone on the highway. But now he couldn't control the car. He was off the blacktop and on the soft shoulder. All this in seconds, and then his own car lights were sweeping crazily off the highway, and a tree loomed straight ahead. There was a grinding, searing crash, then darkness closed down on Danny.

He awoke in a hospital three days later. He had a broken shoulder, a ruptured stomach where a spoke from the steering wheel had penetrated, a concussion, four teeth knocked out, and a back that would eventually call for three operations. The total cost to his parents would run into thousands of dollars. He would lose two years of school.

Ricco was not so lucky. His car rocketed one hundred feet to the bottom of the canyon, landing on huge boulders. Death was instantaneous.

Reader Response

"Chicken!" is a story about two young people who allow themselves to be led into doing something extremely foolish, something that Danny would regret for the rest of his life and that cost Ricco life itself.

There is a bit of Danny and Ricco in all of us. In your response journal, write about some foolish action or decision on the part of someone you know or on your own part. Include these three key points:

a. Identify the person you are talking about.

b. Describe the act or decision.

c. Note the results.

Active Reading

The Don James story carries the reader smoothly from the dare to the action to the destruction. The sentences themselves help to build the excitement. Review the selection noting how the sentences vary: Some are short, saucy questions. Some are emotion-filled exclamations. Others are lengthy declarative sentences taking up a full paragraph of the narrative. Some begin with modifiers. Identify at least one exclamatory, one interrogative, and one declarative sentence by labeling each in the margin.

Studying Model Writing Techniques

Sentence Variety by Types

REMEMBER! All sorts of choices are open to you in the kinds of words and sentences you use to express yourself.

A variety of sentence types and styles is available to you in your writing. By making choices among these styles, you can add sparkle and emphasis to your writing.

Here are some of the choices available to you:

1. You can use declarative sentences.

Most people hate filling in forms.

2. You can use interrogative sentences.

Do you hate filling in forms?

3. You can use exclamatory sentences.

Down with forms!

4. You can use imperative sentences.

   Fill in the form.

5. You can use sentences in the active voice (the subject does the action) or the passive voice (the subject receives the action).

   ACTIVE: *Nearly everybody has to fill in forms.*
   PASSIVE: *Forms have to be filled in by nearly everybody.*

6. You can sometimes reverse the usual order and use sentences in which the subject follows the verb.

   Finally came the forms that had to be completed.
   There before me was a form.

7. As you have learned, you can use sentences that begin with a modifier.

   ADJECTIVE: Fearful, *the man began to run.*
   ADVERB: Unexpectedly, *the man began to run.*
   PREPOSITIONAL PHRASE: In panic, *the man began to run.*
   PARTICIPIAL PHRASE: Fearing the worst, *the man began to run.*
   ADVERB CLAUSE: As panic seized him, *the man began to run.*

Exercise 1   From the literary selection by Don James, locate an example of each of the following types of sentences.

1. Declarative sentence

_____

2. Interrogative sentence

_____

3. Exclamatory sentence

_____

4. Imperative sentence

_____

5. Sentence beginning with modifier

_____

Exercise 2   The following exercise will give you some practice with sentence variety. Read each item carefully, and follow the directions.

1. Rewrite the following sentence, changing it from declarative to interrogative.

   Peanut butter is good for you.

_____

2. Rewrite the following sentence, changing it from interrogative to imperative.

   Do you practice every day?

   _____

3. Rewrite the following sentence, changing it from interrogative to exclamatory.

   Does he eat six eggs and a steak for breakfast?

   _____

4. Rewrite the following sentence, changing the verb from passive voice to active voice.

   The house was damaged badly by the fire.

   _____

5. Rewrite the following sentence, changing the verb from active voice to passive voice.

   The fish took the bait.

   _____

6. Rearrange the following sentence so that it begins with the italicized adjective.

   The *furious* girl slammed the door shut.

   _____

7. Rearrange the following sentence so that it begins with the italicized adverb.

   He pleaded for forgiveness *tearfully*.

   _____

8. Rearrange the following sentence so that it begins with the italicized participial phrase.

   The surf, *whipped by the winds*, became dangerously rough.

   _____

9. Rearrange the following sentence so that it begins with the italicized prepositional phrase.

   She lowered the rope *with great care*.

   _____

10. Rewrite the following sentence, changing it from interrogative to declarative.

    Are we fooling ourselves?

    _____

Exercise 3   Now try writing completely original sentences according to the directions given. Try to make each sentence lively and interesting.

1. Write a declarative sentence about a member of your family.

   _____

   _____

2. Write a declarative sentence about a decision you had to make recently.

_____

_____

3. Write an interrogative sentence about something you like.

_____

_____

_____

4. Write an interrogative sentence about someone you don't like.

_____

_____

_____

5. Write an exclamatory sentence about something recently in the news.

_____

_____

_____

6. Write an exclamatory sentence about a place.

_____

_____

_____

7. Write an imperative sentence about clothing.

_____

_____

_____

8. Write an imperative sentence about crime.

_____

_____

9. Write a sentence in the passive voice about music or dancing.

_____

_____

_____

10. Write a sentence about money in which the subject follows the verb.

_____

_____

Response

Modeling

After studying the literary selection and completing the exercises, you should be able to recognize the importance of a variety of sentence types in a piece of writing. Turn back to your response journal entry about a foolish act or decision. Reread what you wrote. Of course, you wrote informally, so you were not thinking about sentence variety and all the other fine points of style. That's okay. But now look at your sentence structure. Identify the types of sentences you have used. Do you tend to use only one type? Think about ways you could change some sentences to create greater variety—and thereby greater interest—in your writing. Then try to revise a few sentences to generate variety, not just for the sake of variety but also for the sake of emphasis.

> ## Computer Hint
>
> Try rearranging your journal entry's sentences as if they were an exercise. Number each sentence and use the hard return to generate the exercise items. Then study each sentence independently. Such an approach should help you see how much—or how little—variety your sentences demonstrate.

Writing

Use the ideas from your response journal to write a narrative about a foolish action or decision on the part of someone you know or on your own part. Although you may choose and develop your own subject, you may wish to follow the suggestions here:

In your introductory paragraph, you will want to set the stage by identifying the person and telling something about the circumstances leading up to the act or decision. For instance, if you are writing about yourself, you might begin your first paragraph something like this:

> It is true I was only thirteen at the time. Nevertheless, I should have known better. Why didn't I? I suppose because it was my first baby-sitting job, and I got carried away with an unfamiliar sense of freedom and power. Then, too, there was little Jack, a spoiled and mischievous brat if there ever was one.

You will notice the advantages of an introductory paragraph such as this. It plunges right into the tale you have to tell without wasting words. It arouses the reader's interest. The reader wants to know what happened.

You will then want to devote two or more paragraphs to relating chronologically the events you have to tell about. Give a step-by-step account, keeping it simple and clear. Divide your paragraphs at some appropriate turning point in the course of events. In many cases, the events immediately leading up to the foolish act or decision will make one paragraph. The events immediately resulting from the foolish act or decision will make another.

Your final paragraph should bring your composition to an appropriate conclusion. You may wish to draw a lesson or moral from the tale you have told, or you may want to make some other summary observation. Here is one example, out of many possible ones, of a concluding paragraph.

> That happened a long time ago, when I was thirteen. I have never forgotten it, but at last I have gotten it off my chest. Maybe I'll be able to forget it now. On the other hand, maybe it is better that I never forget it!

As you develop this first draft, concentrate on subject matter: your main ideas and their supporting details. You will revise and polish later.

COMPUTER HINT

Don't spend lots of time worrying about the order in which details appear in your first draft. You can use the move command to rearrange sentences or whole paragraphs.

REVISION

Now that you have finished the first draft of your narrative about a foolish action or decision, you are ready to revise. In the revision process, we will focus on organization, chains of meaning, and proofreading details. Use the material as a model for your own revision process.

Checking Organization

Contrast

REMEMBER!   Organized thinking is essential in composition writing.

Writers often use contrast to convey messages. James sets up a number of contrasts in "Chicken!" For instance, early in the story, he contrasts the smile with the tenseness, Ricco's sharp challenge with Danny's quiet answer, Danny's hesitation with Florence's sudden fear, Florence's shaking her head with Danny's nodding. Even the raceway is a set of contrasts: a straight stretch, curves, hills, and a hair-raising half mile along the edge of a hundred-foot-deep canyon. The following exercises will provide you with practice in handling contrast.

Exercise 4   Find five more examples of contrast from "Chicken!"

1. _____

2. _____

3. _____

4. _____

5. _____

Exercise 5 For each numbered word below, there is an opposite in the right-hand column. In the spaces write the best opposites that you can select from the list. The first word is done for you as an example.

1. cautious _careless_

2. create _____

3. dead _____

4. failure _____

5. float _____

6. happy _____

7. lose _____

8. sell _____

9. start _____

10. stretch _____

alive
buy
careless
destroy
find
finish
sad
shrink
sink
success

Exercise 6 In each group of four words, circle the two that are opposites.

1. clumsy   graceful   large   upright

2. change   punish   reward   think

3. late   often   seldom   when

4. hurry   shout   take   whisper

5. familiar   fortunate   prompt   strange

6. gone   valuable   vary   worthless

7. complicated   few   simple   optimistic

8. coward   champion   fellow   hero

9. hopeful   modern   polite   rude

10. break   find   mix   repair

11. always   fast   never   past

12. bolt   clap   danger   safety

13. close   follow   jump   lead

14. known   plentiful   poor   scarce

15. corrupt   dark   mellow   pure

Exercise 7 Select your own opposites. In the space provided, write the best opposite you can think of for each of the following words. The first is done for you as an example.

1. asleep _awake_

2. back _____

3. beginning _____

4. dirty _____

5. down _____

6. guilty _____

7. noise _____

8. none _____

9. old _____

10. on _____

11. small _____

12. smooth _____

13. take	_____	17. temporary	_____
14. top	_____	18. boring	_____
15. yes	_____	19. hollow	_____
16. ask	_____	20. forget	_____

Modeling

Look now at your first draft about a foolish act or decision. Can you find places in which the use of contrast will build suspense, clarify your message, or in some way better color the meaning and impact of your message? Ask a peer editor for his or her response. Make revisions accordingly.

Checking Chains of Meaning

Similarity and Sameness

REMEMBER! In composition writing, sentences are not individual or isolated. Instead, the thought is carried along from sentence to sentence in a chain of meaning.

In the previous units, you learned about transition words and phrases, words that repeat meanings, and pronouns. These are the language forms by which meaning is carried through a sequence of sentences.

These language forms are the outward expression of underlying thought forms. Thought forms are the raw material out of which is forged the chain of meaning in sentence sequences. In the exercises that follow, you will begin to learn about thought forms.

One of the important thought forms that shape sentence sequence is *similarity* or *sameness*. That is, the same kind of idea, at the same level of importance, occurs in each sentence of the sequence. To illustrate, study sentence sequences *a*, *b*, *c*, and *d* below. Can you see that the underlying thought form of *a* and *b* is similarity or sameness?

a. Nevada is sparsely populated. Its desert wastes reach everywhere. Its ground is barren and unproductive.

b. International understanding is essential. International cooperation is necessary for survival.

Compare the preceding examples with the ones that follow. You can see that in the following sentences, the underlying thought form is **not** similarity or sameness.

c. I prefer to write with a black ballpoint pen. Many students I know feel otherwise. One friend of mine has such bad handwriting she will use only a typewriter.

d. Many people think that dragons are extinct creatures. Of course, they are wrong. Dragons are a figment of human imagination.

The underlying thought form for the three sentences in items *c* and *d* is *not* similarity or sameness because the second and third sentences express ideas which contradict or negate the first.

Exercise 8 In seven of the following sentence sequences, the underlying thought form is similarity or sameness. Study each sequence carefully. Place a check beside each sentence sequence in which you feel the underlying thought form is sameness or similarity.

_____ 1. She is an excellent swimmer. Her tennis is superb. She is one of the best golfers in the school.

_____ 2. The stars shone bright and clear. The moon was a great white globe. The night air was still.

_____ 3. Shakespeare wrote many great plays. The one generally recognized as the finest is *Hamlet*. Personally, I prefer *Romeo and Juliet*.

_____ 4. Cats are independent animals. They do as they please when they please. They never truly recognize a master.

_____ 5. The applicant was neatly dressed. Her manner was confident. She spoke in a quiet, self-assured voice.

_____ 6. Education qualifies a person for a better-paying job. Educated people are, generally, better able to handle their personal lives. The responsibilities of good citizenship are more likely to be met effectively by those who have some education.

_____ 7. Careful driving will reduce gas consumption. Careful driving will save countless lives.

_____ 8. Gertrude Ederle was the first woman to swim the English Channel. Jackie Robinson broke the race barrier in major league baseball. Roger Bannister ran an unprecedented mile in less than four minutes.

_____ 9. The Civil War was characterized by many terrible battles. The most famous of these is Gettysburg. The battle at Shiloh, though not so well known, was perhaps more appalling.

_____ 10. Writing a composition is far from easy. Yet, the well-done finished product affords great personal satisfaction.

Exercise 9 In some of the following sentence sequences from "Chicken!" the underlying thought form is similarity or sameness. Study each sequence carefully. Place a check beside each sentence sequence in which you feel the underlying thought form is sameness or similarity.

_____ 1. A lookout from there could see almost ten miles down a straightaway toward the mill. When the highway was clear, he could signal for the start by flashing his headlight toward the waiting racers.

_____ 2. "He's dirty. You know he is. It's not that you aren't a better driver—it's just that . . . well, you can't trust him."

_____ 3. Both drivers clamped hard on the gas again. The speedometer needles climbed. . . . Danny felt the steering wheel grow slick under the sweat of his hands.

_____ 4. The fenders touched and the cars bounced apart. Danny felt his car sway, and he fought the wheel.

_____ 5. Ricco no longer was beside him, and he was strangely alone on the highway. But now he couldn't control the car.

Exercise 10   Now try some original work in writing sentence sequences whose underlying thought form is sameness or similarity. To each of the following sentences, add one or two sentences of your own to form a sequence whose underlying thought form is sameness or similarity.

1. Her eyes were the deepest brown.

2. Bees give us honey.

3. Canada is a good neighbor on our northern border.

4. The refrigerator is one basic kitchen appliance.

5. A house can be built of brick.

6. We all need faith.

7. The roots of the tree spread underground in a great circle.

8. Summer is the time for picnics.

9. Reading offers relaxation.

_____

_____

_____

10. The dove is a symbol of peace.

_____

_____

_____

Modeling

Study your first draft. Can you create better chains of meaning by developing sentence sequences whose underlying thought form is sameness or similarity? Ask a peer or peers for their response. Revise as necessary to generate emphasis in this manner.

Proofreading

As you proofread for errors in spelling and punctuation, you should also take note of the two common errors emphasized here for your attention: agreement of pronouns with antecedents and clear reference of pronouns. The exercises that follow will help you to recognize and avoid these errors in your writing.

Agreement of Pronouns with Antecedents

Pronouns are important words in the structure of sentences. By taking the place of a noun or another pronoun, a pronoun makes it possible to avoid monotonous repetition.

Jo Ellen demonstrated Jo Ellen's ice-skating ability to Jo Ellen's coach.
Jo Ellen demonstrated _her_ ice-skating ability to _her_ coach.

The mountain soared above us. The mountain's lower slopes were thick with timber. The mountain's snow-capped peak was bare of vegetation.

The mountain soared above us. _Its_ lower slopes were thick with timber. _Its_ snow-capped peak was bare of vegetation.

The morning is a fine morning. The morning is clear and warm.
The morning is a fine _one_. _It_ is clear and warm.

There are five kinds of pronouns: _personal, demonstrative, indefinite, relative,_ and _interrogative._

PERSONAL: I, me, we, us, you, he, him, she, her, it, they, them

_I_ ate the cake.
The cake was eaten by _me_.

_We_ ate the cake.
The cake was eaten by _us_.

You ate the cake.
The cake was eaten by _you_.

He ate the cake.
The cake was eaten by *him*.

She ate the cake.
The cake was eaten by *her*.

Everybody had a piece of *it*.

They ate the cake.
The cake was eaten by *them*.

DEMONSTRATIVE: this, these, that, those

This is the road.
Roberto gave me *these*.

That is Susan in the canoe.
Those are the shoes I bought.

INDEFINITE: each, either, both, neither, some, any, such, none, other, another, one, all, several, few, many, anybody, anyone, everybody, everyone, somebody, someone, nobody, no one

The paintings are attractive. *Each* has its merits.
The dresses are lovely. *Either* (or *Any*, *All*, or *Both*) will do.
I expected twelve letters. I received *none* (or *one* or *some*).
I expected many guests. *Few* (or *None*) came.
I expected a few guests. *Many* (or *All*) came.
The piece of cake was small. I ate *another* (or *several*).

RELATIVE: who, whose, whom, which, that

It is you *who* are wrong.
Maria Montoya, *whom* you met, will be hired.
The tenor, *whose* voice was lovely, was roundly applauded.
We have one cow, *which* we prize highly.
This is the house *that* Jack built.

INTERROGATIVE: who, whom, whose, which, what

Who will cast the first stone?
Whom have they elected?
Whose dime is this?
Which is the road we must take?
What are you going to say?

Pronouns have an antecedent, the noun or pronoun that the pronoun refers to. Every pronoun must agree with its antecedent in person and number. For example, which is correct?

It is I who am responsible.
It is I who is responsible.

To decide which is correct, look for the antecedent of the pronoun *who*. The antecedent is *I*. *I* is in the first person and is singular in number. Therefore, *who* is in the first person and is singular in number. Therefore, the verb should be first person singular—*am*, not *is*.

Which is correct?

The roads that leads to the shore are washed out.
The roads that lead to the shore are washed out.

To decide which is correct, look for the antecedent of the pronoun *that*. The antecedent is *roads*. *Roads* is third person plural. Therefore, *that* is third person plural. Therefore, the verb should be third person plural—*lead*, not *leads*.

Exercise 11 Decide which is correct. Cross out the incorrect form.

1. These are the books that (*deal, deals*) with social problems.

2. All you who (*are, is*) ready can go.

3. All of these men care how they look, but each (*is, are*) dressed appropriately for the job.

4. She is the only one of those women who (*play, plays*) bridge well.

5. It is up to me, who (*am, is*) in charge here, how much money should be spent.

Exercise 12 Decide which is correct. Cross out the incorrect form.

1. Although the average woman wants to have a career, (*she, they*) sometimes finds (*her, their*) ambition frustrated because of social prejudices.

2. After reading his argument in favor of national health care, I found I was not convinced by (*it, them*).

3. The prehistoric ancestors of today's horse were not known for (*its, their*) enormous size.

4. The male elephant, with (*its, their*) large ivory tusks, has been threatened with extinction.

5. The box, containing vast riches, (*its, their*) contents strewn about, lay smashed in the road.

The following pronouns are singular: *one, everybody, anybody, each*. When these pronouns act as an antecedent, the related pronouns should also be singular. If the gender is unknown, current practice recommends using the phrase *his or her* rather than the traditional *his*.

WRONG: *Everybody has* their *faults.*
RIGHT: *Everybody has* his or her *faults.*

WRONG: *If anybody wishes to leave,* they *may do so now.*
RIGHT: *If anybody wishes to leave,* he or she *may do so now.*

WRONG: *Each of us must lead* their *own life.*
RIGHT: *Each of us must lead* his or her *own life.*

Remember that two singular nouns connected by *or* are considered singular and will act as a singular antecedent.

WRONG: *Marie or Coretta has forgotten their suitcase.*
RIGHT: *Marie or Coretta has forgotten* her *suitcase.*

WRONG: *My father or my uncle will lend me their car.*
RIGHT: *My father or my uncle will lend me* his *car.*

Pronouns and antecedents must agree in person and number. Be consistent in your use of pronouns and antecedents.

WRONG: *If one drinks too much coffee, it will speed up* your *heart, make* us *nervous, and keep* you *awake.*
RIGHT: *If* one *drinks too much coffee, it will speed up* one's *heart, make* one *nervous, and keep* one *awake.*
RIGHT: *If* you *drink too much coffee, it will speed up* your *heart, make* you *nervous, and keep* you *awake.*
RIGHT: *If* we *drink too much coffee, it will speed up* our *hearts, make* us *nervous, and keep* us *awake.*

Exercise 13 Rewrite each of the following sentences to correct any error in agreement between pronoun and antecedent.

1. Rosa or Sue will lend us their bike.

_____

2. Each of us has their job to do.

_____

3. If one has a serious problem, you should seek advice from a trusted person, who may be able to help us.

_____

_____

4. Everybody is requested to bring their own lunch.

_____

_____

5. The tiger or the lion is scheduled to do their act next.

_____

_____

Clear Reference of Pronouns

Look at these sentences:

a. If the baby is not able to digest the milk, it should be boiled. (What should be boiled—the milk or the baby?)

b. My father and mother told us not to read the books because they were too old-fashioned. (What were old-fashioned—the books or father and mother?)

c. Tom told Bill his income-tax refund had come in the mail. (Whose refund had come—Tom's or Bill's?)

When a pronoun has two or more possible antecedents, the antecedent is said to be *ambiguous*. A pronoun must have one clear antecedent to avoid confusion. Here are the three sentences improved.

    a. The milk should be boiled if the baby is not able to digest it.

    b. My father and mother told us that the books were too old-fashioned to read.

    c. "Your income-tax refund has come in the mail," Tom told Bill.

Look at these sentences.

    d. His hands were chained, but they were removed at the door.

    e. Though my sisters are doctors, it has never appealed to me.

    f. She couldn't understand how to cook the meat until I wrote it out.

You can see that these sentences are unclear. The problem is that the pronouns have no stated antecedent, only one that is vaguely suggested. A pronoun must have a definite, stated antecedent. Here are the three sentences improved.

    d. His hands were in chains, which were removed at the door.

    e. Though my sisters are doctors, the profession has never appealed to me.

    f. She couldn't understand how to cook the meat until I wrote out the instructions.

Exercise 14   Each of the following sentences has either an ambiguous antecedent or no definite antecedent. Revise each sentence to eliminate the error.

  1. He had been vaccinated against typhoid, but *it* didn't protect him.

  2. We visited Japan and discovered that *they* are like Americans in many respects.

  3. If the practice session and the concert are scheduled at the same time, I will have to miss *it*.

  4. When patients consult their doctors, *they* should show some personal interest.

  5. Roberto has known my brother since *he* was five years old.

6. The streets are awfully dirty, and *they* should do something about cleaning them up.

_____

_____

7. She talked a lot about the techniques of horsemanship, although she had never actually ridden *one*.

_____

_____

8. The mother complained to the daughter about *her* inability to concentrate.

_____

_____

9. The township is not getting the snow off the roads promptly, *which* makes everyone furious.

_____

_____

10. Sheila told Phyllis that *she* was getting a raise.

_____

_____

> ## COMPUTER HINT
>
> Some computer style checkers will point out agreement errors, but most will not recognize unclear reference. Use a style checker to your advantage, but keep in mind that you must know the grammar, mechanics, and usage rules as well. And sometimes style checkers will point out "errors" that aren't!

Modeling

After you have gone through the exercises, return to the literary model. Notice the frequent use of pronouns. Check each pronoun's antecedent. Does each pronoun have a clear reference? Consider these model sentences with personal pronouns italicized:

a. "*I'm* not chicken," Danny said. "*I* can take *you* in that car of *yours* anytime."

b. For a second Danny hesitated. *He* glanced at Florence, *his* girl, and *she* suddenly appeared to be frightened.

c. From the corner of *his* eye, *he* saw Ricco's headlights cast a light toward the far side of the canyon, and a few seconds later *he* dimly heard a faraway crash.

When you have finished the exercises and studied the model, give your composition a final proofreading.

Peer or Self-Editing Guidelines

Before you prepare a final copy of your narrative about a foolish act or decision, ask a peer or peers to read it and use the following guidelines for offering suggestions. Or use the guidelines as a means of self-evaluation.

	very well	1	2	3	4	poorly
1. How well does the composition demonstrate variety by types of sentences?						
2. How well does the writer use contrast for emphasis?						
3. How well does the writer use similarity and sameness to create chains of meaning?						
4. How well has the writer made pronouns agree with their antecedents?						
5. How well has the writer given clear references to pronouns?						

The Final Draft: Sharing

As you prepare your final draft for the publication stage, take into consideration your peers' suggestions and/or your self-evaluation based on the guidelines above. Add a title. Then read again to check for final details.

Unit 5

A Description of a Trip

PREWRITING

Reading the Literature

Master storytellers create pictures with only a few details. Truman Capote, author of "A Ride through Spain," describes settings so well that readers often feel they are a part of them. As you read to enjoy the following literary selection, try to visualize the setting.

from A RIDE THROUGH SPAIN by Truman Capote

Certainly the train was old. The seats sagged like the jowls of a bulldog, windows were out and strips of adhesive held together those that were left; in the corridor a prowling cat appeared to be hunting mice, and it was not unreasonable to assume his search would be rewarded.

Slowly, as though the engine were harnessed to elderly coolies, we crept out of Granada. The southern sky was as white and burning as a desert; there was one cloud, and it drifted like a traveling oasis.

We were going to Algeciras, a Spanish seaport facing the coast of Africa. In our compartment there was a middle-aged Australian wearing a soiled linen suit; he had tobacco-colored teeth and his fingernails were unsanitary. Presently, he informed us that he was a ship's doctor. It seemed curious, there on the dry, dour plains of Spain, to meet someone connected with the sea. Seated next to him there were two women, a mother and daughter. The mother was an overstuffed, dusty woman with sluggish, disapproving eyes and a faint mustache. The focus for her disapproval fluctuated; first, she eyed me rather strongly because, as the sunlight fanned brighter, waves of heat blew through the broken windows and I had removed my jacket—which she considered, perhaps rightly, discourteous. Later on, she took a dislike to the young soldier who also occupied our compartment. The soldier and the woman's not very discreet daughter, a buxom girl with the scrappy features of a prizefighter, seemed to have agreed to flirt. Whenever the wandering cat appeared at our door, the daughter pretended to be frightened, and the soldier would gallantly shoo the cat into the corridor: this byplay gave them frequent opportunity to touch each other.

The young soldier was one of many on the train. With their tasseled caps set at snappy angles, they hung about in the corridors smoking sweet black cigarettes and laughing confidentially. They seemed to be enjoying themselves, which apparently was wrong of them, for whenever an officer appeared, the soldiers would stare fixedly out the windows, as though enraptured by the landslides of red rock, the olive fields, and stern stone mountains. Their officers were dressed for a parade, many ribbons, much brass; and some wore gleaming, improbable swords strapped to their sides. They did not mix with the soldiers, but sat together in a first-class compartment, looking bored and rather like unemployed actors. It was a blessing, I suppose, that something finally happened to give them a chance at rattling their swords.

The compartment directly ahead was taken over by one family: a delicate, attenuated, exceptionally elegant man with a mourning ribbon sewn around his sleeve, and, traveling with him, six thin, summery girls, presumably his daughters. They were beautiful, the father and his children, all of them, and in the same way: hair that had a dark shine, lips the color of pimentos, eyes like sherry. The soldiers would glance into their compartment, then look away. It was as if they had seen straight into the sun.

Whenever the train stopped, the man's two youngest daughters would descend from the carriage and stroll under the shade of parasols. They enjoyed many lengthy promenades, for the train spent the greatest part of our journey standing still. No one appeared to be exasperated by this except myself. Several passengers seemed to have friends at every station with whom they could sit around a fountain and gossip long and lazily. One old woman was met by different little groups in a dozen-odd towns—between these encounters she wept with such abandon that the Australian doctor became alarmed; why no, she said, there was nothing he could do, it was just that seeing all her relatives made her so happy.

At each stop cyclones of barefooted women and somewhat naked children ran beside the train sloshing earthen jars of water and furiously squalling *Agua! Agua!* For two pesetas you could buy a whole basket of dark runny figs, and there were trays of curious white-coated candy doughnuts that looked as though they should be eaten by young girls wearing Communion dresses. Toward noon, having collected a bottle of wine, a loaf of bread, a sausage and a cheese, we were prepared for lunch. Our companions in the compartment were hungry, too. Packages were produced, wine uncorked, and for a while there was a pleasant, almost graceful festiveness. The soldier shared a pomegranate with the girl, the Australian told an amusing story, the witch-eyed mother pulled a paper-wrapped fish from her bosom and ate it with a glum relish.

Afterwards, everyone was sleepy; the doctor went so solidly to sleep that a fly meandered undisturbed over his open-mouthed face. Stillness etherized the whole train; in the next compartment the lovely girls leaned loosely, like six exhausted geraniums; even the cat had ceased to prowl, and lay dreaming in the corridor. We had climbed higher, the train moseyed across a plateau of rough yellow wheat, then between the granite walls of deep ravines where wind, moving down from the mountains, quivered in strange, thorny trees. Once, at a parting in the trees, there was something I'd wanted to see, a castle on a hill, and it sat there like a crown.

Reader Response

Think about the narrator's trip from Granada to Algeciras. Let his experiences remind you of a trip of your own. Your trip may be one to a far-off place—a distant city, a vacation spot, or a foreign country. Or, it may be a more ordinary trip—to a supermarket or department store for shopping; to the beach, a pool, or lakeside on a summer's day; to a doctor's or dentist's office, or to a hospital; to a football game or other sports event; to a school dance or a discotheque; to a circus or fair. Or you may choose an imaginary trip, one that you daydream about.

In your response journal, freewrite about your trip. Write informally, as if you were talking to yourself, about the place and the people. Describe both.

Active Reading

In writing about a train ride across Spain, Truman Capote brings the setting and the people to life by his sharp and selective powers of observation. He briefly and precisely describes the train's sagging seats, the windows, the prowling cat, and the slow pace, as though it were "harnessed to elderly coolies," instead of to an engine. That is all, and we know the whole train as though we were on it.

About the doctor, he tells us of the soiled linen suit, tobacco-stained teeth, unsanitary fingernails. These few key details not only give us the doctor's appearance but also tell us all we might want to know about his character and life. These details have the power of suggestion.

Review the literary selection. Underline words that describe the Spanish landscape. Underline words that describe the young soldier.

Studying Model Writing Techniques

REMEMBER! All sorts of choices are open to you in the kinds of words and sentences you use to express yourself.

Part I: Diction to Create Unity of Setting

When you speak or write, you make many choices in the words you decide to use. The particular choice of words made by a writer is called **diction.** In the exercises that follow, you will add to the techniques you have already learned for using diction more effectively.

Look at the following list. What setting is suggested? Can you add three items to the list that also suggest this setting?

rolling surf	frisbee players	_____
seaweed	salty breeze	_____
soaring gulls	low tide	_____

The words on this list evoke a particular setting—a seashore or beach. Even as a mere list, without sentences, these words suggest to your mind images of the seashore, and the mind adds other images to complete the setting.

Note that this vocabulary and the setting it suggests could appear in many different kinds of composition. You may be giving reasons for your enjoying the seashore. You may be narrating an incident, such as your first attempt at surfing. You may be complaining about pollution of the seashore environment. You may be telling about your first meeting with someone who became close to you.

Using carefully chosen words to suggest a single setting will strengthen your writing.

Exercise 1 Find Capote's carefully chosen words that describe the Spanish countryside setting. List them below.

_____

_____

_____

Exercise 2 Write an original, interesting sentence sequence of three to five sentences in which you make use of some of the words from the seashore list.

_____

_____

_____

_____

Exercise 3 Here are five lists of words and phrases, each suggesting a specific setting. Add three words or phrases of your own to each list to make the setting more complete.

1. Setting: Automotive Repair Shop

   grimy waiting-room chairs   _____
   grease-stained attendants   _____
   oil cans   _____
   hydraulic lift

2. Setting: Cafeteria

   counter   _____
   dishes   _____
   limp sandwiches   _____
   crowded tables

3. Setting: Avenue

   shoppers   _____
   store windows   _____
   litter baskets   _____
   traffic

4. Setting: Dentist's Office

   high-speed drill   _____
   chair   _____
   light   _____
   steel probes

5. Setting: Office

word processors
computers
copiers
fax machines

_____

_____

_____

Exercise 4   Now choose one of the five lists from Exercise 3. Write an interesting, original sequence of three to five sentences. Use several words or phrases from the list to suggest a specific setting.

_____

_____

_____

_____

_____

_____

Part II: Diction to Create Unity of Mood

Look at the following sentence sequence.

> Have you ever walked through a great forest? The brown, sturdy columns of trees stand strong and timeless. The spread of soft carpet below is balanced by the leafy ceiling overhead. Nature's design is serene and orderly here.

Did you notice that the diction of these sentences creates a single **mood** or psychological atmosphere? A strong mood of order and dependability is created by such words as _brown, sturdy, columns, strong, timeless, balanced, design, serene,_ and _orderly._

Other words could also have been included to add to the same mood:

oak   eternal
sphere   symmetry

Add three words of your own that would contribute to the psychological mood of order and dependability.

_____

_____

_____

Using words carefully chosen to suggest a single mood, or psychological atmosphere, will strengthen your writing.

Exercise 5 Study the following paragraph from the Capote selection. Underline the words that help create the single psychological mood about the soldiers. Then name the mood.

> The young soldier was one of many on the train. With their tasseled caps set at snappy angles, they hung about in the corridors smoking sweet black cigarettes and laughing confidentially. They seemed to be enjoying themselves, which apparently was wrong of them, for whenever an officer appeared, the soldiers would stare fixedly out the windows, as though enraptured by the landslides of red rock, the olive fields, and stern stone mountains.

Mood: _____

Exercise 6 Here are five lists of words, each suggesting a single mood. Add three words of your own to each list.

1. *Mood*: Disorder; uncertainty; chaos

fragments	muddle	_____
ruins	perish	
short-lived	vanishing	_____
unpredictable	anarchy	_____

2. *Mood*: Abundance; prosperity

fertile	pipelines	_____
gold	bonanza	
rainbow	honey	_____
fruit	purple	_____

3. *Mood*: Faith; serenity

glow	meditate	_____
candle	haven	
shrine	temple	_____
tonic	inspire	_____

4. *Mood*: Depression; sadness

silent	gloomy	_____
ache	whimpering	
rain	weeping	_____
alone	darkness	_____

5. *Mood*: Energy; vitality

electric	power	_____
sparkle	keen	
crisp	stride	_____
surf	laughter	_____

Exercise 7 Can you make a list of your own? Choose any one of the following moods, and make a list of at least ten words to help create the mood.

luxury	power; strength
courage	celebration
serenity	fear

Mood: _____

1. _____   6. _____

2. _____   7. _____

3. _____   8. _____

4. _____   9. _____

5. _____   10. _____

Exercise 8 Choose any one of the six lists of words from Exercises 6 and 7 that suggest a single mood. Write a sentence sequence of three to five sentences in which you use several of the words from the list.

_____

_____

_____

_____

_____

_____

_____

_____

_____

RESPONSE

Modeling

Now that you have studied how diction maintains the unity of setting and mood in the literary selection and in the exercises, turn to your journal entry about a trip. Reread what you wrote. Think about what your reader needs in order to see the setting. Think about the mood you want to create. Do you want the reader to see this trip as a disaster, a dream come true, a fluke, a surprise, a well-planned joyous event, a happy-turned-miserable occurrence, or something else? When you decide, use words the way Capote does so that you clarify the setting and clearly establish the mood. You may need to add or substitute new words to create the desired effect.

Writing

Use your journal entry and subsequent additions as the basis for a description of a familiar setting. In this composition, see how well you can use Capote-like descriptive writing techniques to tell about a trip of your own.

In writing this composition, remember to be selective. Carefully choose a few key details of the place and a few key details about people. Remember to try to make each detail count by being as exact and vivid as you can and by selecting only details that are important. If you are successful, you will be using the power of suggestion to say far more than the few words you use.

You will probably want to devote your first paragraph to key details about the overall setting or destination. Try to select details that establish a single mood, feeling, or atmosphere. For example, Capote's details all contribute to the strangely decrepit, run-down character of the train. Or, if you are writing about the dentist's office you may wish to select details that help to establish a mood of fear. You could begin this way:

> On the tray lay a dozen steel instruments. Several had needlelike points bent at various tortured angles. Others had cutting-chisel edges of various widths. They were all designed to excavate various types of holes in living flesh. Two pairs of massive pliers were threatening engines of destruction. Wads of cotton gauze readied for flowing blood lay on the counter. A cold, glaring overhead lamp glinted on the metal surfaces. The hospital smell of disinfectants tainted the air.

You will probably want to devote each of your second and third paragraphs to a few persons important in the setting you have chosen. Once again, use a few key details to say a lot.

> The brisk, white-clad assistant sat me in the chair, lowering it to a horizontal position. She draped me with a plastic sheet like a corpse in the morgue. The dentist bent over me. The overhead light made a yellow glare on his pale, bald head. Behind his steel-rimmed glasses, his eyes seemed staring and lidless, like a shark's . . .

In your fourth and last paragraph, you will want to bring your composition to a strong, appropriate conclusion. One way of doing this is by relating a final event. For example:

> I stood up on shaky legs, the right half of my lips, tongue, cheek, and palate numb as though they were not there. As I half-listened to some final

instructions about rinsing with salt water, my attention was fixed mainly on my former wisdom tooth, bloody, with what looked like shreds of flesh on the roots, lying on the bloodstained gauze, amidst the bloodstained instruments in disarray on the tray. I opened the door to the reception room. The next patient, a pale young man, jerked his head up, startled, as he heard the door open. I felt pity and smiled a friendly, encouraging smile. But half my mouth was dead. The smile may have looked more like a leer.

There are other ways of bringing your composition to a strong conclusion. Contrast can be effective. For instance, if your composition has been about a lovely summer's day somewhere, in your last paragraph you can write about trudging through deep snow, freezing in icy winds, and remembering the summer trip all the more vividly. If your composition is about a visit to a hospital, you can, by way of conclusion, contrast the atmosphere of the outside world to that of the hospital.

Choose your own setting. Try to decide on a single mood, feeling, or atmosphere that you want to emphasize. Select your details with that single effect in mind.

As you develop this first draft, concentrate on subject matter. Later, you will revise and polish.

REVISION

Now that you have finished the first draft of your description of a trip, you are ready to revise. In the revision process, we will focus on organization, chains of meaning, and proofreading details. Use the material as a model for your own revision process.

Checking Organization

Logical or Natural Order

REMEMBER! Organized thinking is essential in composition writing.

An important skill of organization is the ability to arrange ideas and things in a **logical order.** In these exercises, you will rearrange ideas and things so that they appear in chronological or spatial order or in order of importance.

You are given:

March, February, April, January

You would want to list these items in chronological order:

January, February, March, April

You are given:

leaves, roots, limbs, trunk

You would want to list these items in spatial order; perhaps from bottom to top:

roots, trunk, limbs, leaves

The reverse order (of top to bottom) is also spatial order, as is left to right, right to left, front to back, or back to front.

You are given:

elephant, rabbit, ant, mouse, lion

You would want to list these items in a logical order of importance, perhaps according to size:

ant, mouse, rabbit, lion, elephant

The reverse order (of big to little) is also a logical order of importance.

Exercise 9 Return to "A Ride Through Spain." Determine the order Capote uses in each of these sentences: chronological, spatial, or in order of importance.

1. They were beautiful, the father and his children, all of them, and in the same way: hair that had a dark shine, lips the color of pimentos, eyes like sherry.

   Order: _____

2. The focus of her disapproval fluctuated; first, she eyed me rather strongly. . . . Later on, she took a dislike to the young soldier. . . .

   Order: _____

3. Several passengers seemed to have friends at every station with whom they could sit around a fountain and gossip long and lazily. One old woman was met by different little groups in a dozen-odd towns. . . .

   Order: _____

4. Packages were produced, wine uncorked, and for a while there was a pleasant, almost graceful festiveness.

   Order: _____

5. The soldier shared a pomegranate with the girl, the Australian told an amusing story, the witch-eyed mother pulled a paper-wrapped fish from her bosom and ate it with a glum relish.

   Order: _____

Exercise 10 Use the spaces to the right to rearrange each list in an order that satisfies you. The first one has been done for you as an example.

1. noon   *morning, noon, night* _____
   morning
   night

2. average   _____
   enormous
   large
   tiny

3. soup   _____
   dessert
   appetizer
   main course

78

4. beef
   food
   meat
   sirloin

   _____

5. breeze
   calm
   hurricane
   wind

   _____

6. butter
   eat
   slice
   toast

   _____

7. develop
   focus
   print
   snap

   _____

8. iron
   soil
   wash
   wear

   _____

9. crawl
   sprint
   jog
   walk

   _____

10. family
    mother
    parent
    society

    _____

11. argue
    disagree
    hit
    shove

    _____

12. cardiologist
    doctor
    occupation
    profession

    _____

13. animal
    collie
    dog
    mammal

    _____

14. drop
    lake
    pond
    puddle

    _____

15. awaken
dream
nap
tire

_____

16. paint
plane
sandpaper
saw

_____

17. antibiotic
chemical
medicine
penicillin

_____

18. awaken
depart
dress
wash

_____

19. enclose   seal
fold   stamp
mail   write

_____
_____

20. book   sentence
chapter   syllable
paragraph   word

_____
_____

Modeling

Review your first draft of a description of a trip. Have you presented your ideas in chronological order, spatial order, or in order of importance? Think first about the overall organization. Do you begin at the beginning and move chronologically through the trip? Then think about the details. Do you arrange them in some kind of order? If possible, ask a peer editor for his or her response. Revise as necessary to improve the organization of your description.

Checking Chains of Meaning

Oppositeness

REMEMBER! In composition writing, sentences are not individual or isolated. Instead, the thought is carried along from sentence to sentence in a chain of meaning.

You have learned that similarity or sameness is one of the thought forms that shape the chain of meaning of a sentence sequence. A second such thought form is **oppositeness.** That is, the sequence is formed by first stating an idea and then stating opposite, contradictory, or contrasting ideas.

To illustrate, here is a sentence sequence shaped by oppositeness. Note that the idea of the first sentence is contradicted by the ideas of the second, third, and fourth sentences.

A college education is said to be the pathway to greater earnings. Sometimes the case is otherwise. Some college graduates find great difficulty in locating jobs for which they have prepared themselves. However, much more important, one should look in directions other than the earning of money for the main rewards of a college education. The experience itself is a rich one.

Here is another illustration. Note that the ideas of the first two sentences are in contrast to the ideas of the last two.

It was a neighborhood of great wealth. Its luxurious buildings were manned by doormen in resplendent uniforms, who attended the richly dressed and bejeweled people who came and went in chauffeur-driven limousines and taxicabs. Just a few blocks away was an area of dilapidated, rat-ridden, roach-infested slum houses. On the sidewalks were piles of garbage and litter, among which walked or stood or sat the deprived inhabitants.

Capote, too, uses contrasting sentence sequences. Note the following examples from "A Ride Through Spain":

a. The southern sky was white and burning as a desert; there was one cloud, and it drifted like a traveling oasis.

b. With their tasseled caps set at snappy angles, they hung about in the corridors smoking sweet black cigarettes and laughing confidentially. They seemed to be enjoying themselves, which apparently was wrong of them, for whenever an officer appeared, the soldiers would stare fixedly out the windows, as though enraptured by the landslides of red rock, the olive fields, and stern stone mountains.

c. . . . Between these encounters she wept with such abandon that the Australian doctor became alarmed; why no, she said, there was nothing he could do, it was just that seeing all her relatives made her so happy.

Exercise 11 In seven of the following sentence sequences, the underlying thought form is oppositeness (contradiction or contrast). Study each sequence carefully. Place a check beside each sentence sequence in which the underlying thought form is oppositeness.

_____ **1.** Many people have trouble with mathematics. Nobody knows why. Perhaps some of us are just born with nonmathematical minds.

_____ **2.** Alice was shy and quiet. Her sister Joan was sociable and bubbling with charm.

_____ **3.** Nuclear power was once thought to be a blessing, an inexhaustible source of cheap, clean energy. To many it has become a fearsome peril, an awesome, uncontainable threat to humanity.

_____ **4.** Mr. and Mrs. O'Hara looked forward to their little son's birthday party with joy and anticipation. When it was over, they felt their home had been devastated by an unnatural disaster. They said, "Never again!"

_____ **5.** On one side of the mountain range lie fertile valleys, washed by abundant streams. Groves of fruit trees and acres of vineyards thrive in the valleys. On the other side of the range is a desert, a barren wasteland. Sand, bare rock, and a few scraggly cactuses stretch to the horizon.

_____ 6. The horse is a marvelous animal. The horse's enormous power is clothed in grace and gentleness. Throughout history, humanity has had no greater friend or servant.

_____ 7. We look to government to solve all our economic and ecological ills. But government cannot do everything. The forces that shape our complex society are largely beyond the government's power to control.

_____ 8. Monuments and memorials across all of France honor Napoleon's greatness. The man was a pirate, a plunderer. This would-be conqueror devastated Europe with death and destruction.

_____ 9. Skilled potters are a thrill to watch. They place a blob of clay on the wheel. As the wheel turns, their hands make graceful shapes rise from the lump of clay.

_____ 10. A rocket to the moon is launched. It roars upward with flame and smoke. Everybody applauds. A tiny evergreen seed sprouts. Without a sound the frail young stem thrusts upward through rock and rubble to the air. No one claps.

Exercise 12 Now try your hand at some original writing of sentence sequences whose chain of meaning is shaped by oppositeness. Your sentence sequences can consist of two, three, or four sentences. What should you write about? For ideas, look at the sentences of the previous exercises. For further ideas characterized by oppositeness, contradiction, or contrast, think about hopes or expectations that you or someone you know had where the outcome was different from what was hoped for or expected; think about pairs of people or pairs of places that contrast sharply; think about commonly held beliefs that are not true; think about some recent events in the news that may suggest ideas of oppositeness to you. In the spaces below, write two sentence sequences whose underlying thought form is oppositeness.

1. _____

   _____

   _____

   _____

2. _____

   _____

   _____

   _____

Modeling

In the final paragraph of the literary selection, Capote illustrates the power of opposites. Having clearly described earlier the active, lovely girls, he describes them now as leaning "loosely, like six exhausted geraniums." Even "the cat had ceased to prowl, and lay dreaming in the corridor."

Study your own first draft and, if possible, ask a peer editor to do the same. Can you create opposites where such a contrast will add emphasis to your message? Revise as necessary.

COMPUTER HINT

Although creating oppositeness is more than using antonyms, you may choose to use a computer-disk thesaurus to help you think of opposites. Most thesaurus entries will include antonyms as well as synonyms.

Proofreading

As you proofread for errors in spelling and punctuation, you should also take note of the two common errors emphasized here for your attention: the possessive case of nouns and the possessive case of personal pronouns. The exercises that follow will help you to recognize and avoid these errors in your writing.

The Possessive Case of Nouns

In writing, we frequently want to show that one thing belongs to or is part of another. To illustrate, look especially at the italicized words in each of the following sentences.

The howl of the wolf could be heard in the night.
The howls of the wolves could be heard in the night.

The hat of the woman is attractive.
Hats for women are on sale.

We have another, frequently preferable, choice. Instead of using the words *of* and *for* to show possession, we can use the possessive case.

The wolf's howl could be heard in the night.
The wolves' howls could be heard in the night.

The woman's hat is attractive.
Women's hats are on sale.

The possessive case of all nouns requires the use of an apostrophe (') and an *s*. Many people, however, get confused about where the apostrophe goes and where the *s* goes. That confusion is easily cleared up by two simple rules:

If the *of* or *for* form is used and the word does not end in *s*, add an apostrophe and an *s* ('*s*) to change to the possessive form.

the coat of the child	(child)
the child's coat	(child's)
the coats of the children	(children)
the children's coats	(children's)

If the *of* or *for* form is used and the word already ends in *s*, simply add an apostrophe to change to the possessive form.

the hair of Carlos	(Carlos)
Carlos' hair	(Carlos')
The tails of the monkeys	(monkeys)
the monkeys' tails	(monkeys')

In your writing, if you are not sure of how to write the possessive form of a noun, first mentally put the words into the *of* or *for* form to see whether the noun already ends in *s* or not. Remember that if the noun does not end in *s*, add an apostrophe and an *s*. But if the noun already ends in *s*, add only an apostrophe.

Exercise 13   Rewrite each of the following, using the word *of* or *for* instead of the possessive case of the noun.

> *Example:* the captain's whistle
>
> *the whistle of the captain*

1. cat's paws

   _____

2. Charles Dickens' books

   _____

3. a day's work

   _____

4. two years' memories

   _____

5. the autumn leaves' colors

   _____

6. the students' lounge

   _____

7. the wind's force

   _____

8. the pencils' points

   _____

9. gravity's pull

   _____

10. the countries' traditions

    _____

Exercise 14   Put each of the following into the possessive case. The first two are done for you as examples.

1. the colors of the painting

   the painting's colors
   _____

2. the nose of Pinocchio

   Pinocchio's nose
   _____

3. the salary of Charles

   _____

4. the smell of the gladiolus

   _____

5. the orbits of the planets

   _____

6. the trials of Job

   _____

7. the extinction of the whales

   _____

8. the shoes of the ladies

   _____

9. the shoes of the lady

   _____

10. the fall of the Roman Empire

   _____

Exercise 15   Each of the following sentences has a noun in the possessive case. In seven of the sentences, the possessive case has been written correctly. In three sentences, the possessive case has been written incorrectly. If the possessive case is correct, write a C in the space. If the possessive case is incorrect, rewrite the word correctly in the space.

1. Dolores' new boyfriend is handsome and charming.   _____

2. The medicine's side effects have proved to be dangerous.   _____

3. The police officers' sponsorship of the athletic league was   _____
   approved.

4. The hollie's red berries were bright in the winter sunlight.   _____

5. He did not want to think about the candy's calorie count.   _____

6. What do you think of the country's foreign policy?   _____

7. We laughed at the baby's gurgles.   _____

8. The brushe's bristles had grown soft.   _____

9. The colossus' muscles bulged like mountains.   _____

10. The tycoon's yacht was in the harbor.   _____

The Possessive Case of Personal Pronouns

There is nothing more common than people talking about themselves or to others or about others.

Therefore it is not so strange that the personal pronouns are among the most common words in use. They are also among the most complicated and difficult words in use. When people talk about themselves, the personal pronouns they use are *I, me, my, mine, we, us, our,* and *ours*. When people talk to others, the personal pronouns they use are *you, your,* and *yours*. When people talk about others, the personal pronouns they use are *he, she, it, they, them, their,* and *theirs*. Let us put this information in the form of a table for better understanding.

First Person (Refers to the Speaker)

	Singular	*Plural*
NOMINATIVE	I	we
POSSESSIVE	my, mine	our, ours
OBJECTIVE	me	us

Second Person (Refers to the Person Spoken To)

NOMINATIVE	you	you
POSSESSIVE	your, yours	your, yours
OBJECTIVE	you	you

Third Person (Refers to the Person or Thing Spoken About)

NOMINATIVE	he, she, it	they
POSSESSIVE	his, her, hers, its	their, theirs
OBJECTIVE	him, her, it	them

We are particularly interested, right now, in the possessive case of these personal pronouns.

Note that no apostrophes are used in the possessive case of personal pronouns. These words simply have their own possessive forms, and that fact sometimes causes confusion and errors in writing.

No one has trouble with the possessive forms *my, mine, our, his,* or *her*. No one, for example, ever writes "hi's" or "ou'r."

But people do have trouble with *hers, your, yours, ours, their, theirs,* and, especially, *its*.

The trouble arises with *ours, yours,* and *theirs* because these words are possessive and end in *s*, so there is a temptation to insert an apostrophe. Do not do so.

RIGHT: *The blame is ours.*
WRONG: *The blame is our's.*

RIGHT: *The credit is yours.*
WRONG: *The credit is your's.*

RIGHT: *These tickets are theirs.*
WRONG: *These tickets are their's.*

The trouble with *your, its,* and *their* arises because these words are confused with the contractions of *you are, it is,* and *they are.*

Pronoun + verb	Contraction
you are	you're
it is	it's
they are	they're

The apostrophes in these contractions have nothing to do with possession. The apostrophes stand for an omitted letter.

Possessive	Contraction
you—your	you are—you're
it—its	it is—it's
they—their	they are—they're

Exercise 16 Each of the following sentences contains a form of the personal pronoun in the possessive case or a personal pronoun as part of a contraction. In eight of these sentences, the pronoun has been written correctly. In seven, the pronoun has been written incorrectly. If the pronoun is correct, write a *C* in the space. If the pronoun is incorrect, rewrite it correctly in the space.

1. At last, victory was our's. _____

2. Their diamonds were enormous and glittering. _____

3. It's time to eat. _____

4. Hers was the responsibility to run the meeting. _____

5. You're a fantastic disco dancer. _____

6. They're expected here about five. _____

7. The giraffe stretched it's neck. _____

8. Their's was the satisfaction of seeing justice triumph. _____

9. The horses gobbled they're fodder. _____

10. Seeing its' enemy, the snake poised to strike. _____

11. A chameleon can change its color. _____

12. Is this portfolio yours? _____

13. Have you returned you're book to the library? _____

14. Your being last on the line means you may not get in. _____

15. The clock sounded it's melodious chimes a dozen times. _____

Modeling

After you have gone through the exercises, return to the literary model. Capote uses several possessive nouns and pronouns. Can you spot them? Consider these examples:

a. . . . It was not unreasonable to assume *his* search would be rewarded.

b. In *our* compartment there was a middle-aged Australian. . . .

c. Presently, he informed us that he was a *ship's* doctor.

d. The focus of *her* disapproval fluctuated. . . .

e. . . . I had removed *my* jacket. . . .

f. The soldier and the *woman's* not very discreet daughter . . . seemed to have agreed to flirt.

g. With *their* tasseled caps set at snappy angles, they hung about in the corridors. . . .

h. . . . The *man's* two youngest daughters would descend from the carriage. . . .

When you have finished the exercises and studied the model, give your composition a final proofreading.

Peer or Self-Evaluation Guidelines

Before you prepare a final copy of your description of a trip, ask a peer or peers to read it and use the following guidelines for offering suggestions. Or use the guidelines as a means of self-evaluation.

	very well	1	2	3	4	*poorly*
1. How well does the diction maintain unity of setting?						
2. How well does the diction maintain unity of mood?						
3. How well does the writer use logical or natural order?						
4. How well does the description demonstrate effective chains of meaning, especially in terms of oppositeness?						
5. How well has the writer used the accurate possessive case of nouns and personal pronouns?						

The Final Draft: Sharing

Before you prepare your final draft for the publishing stage, take into consideration your peers' suggestions and/or your self-evaluation based on the guidelines. Add a title. Then read again to check for final details.

COMPUTER HINT

If you use a spell checker, remember that it will check only the accurate spelling of a word—not necessarily the word you need to be using. For instance, a spell checker will see nothing wrong with a sentence that says "He eight a tone of ice cream." All words in the sentence are accurately spelled. Thus, a spell checker will not relieve you of the responsibility for checking your writing.

Unit 6

A Critical Essay on Television Programming

PREWRITING

Reading the Literature

Television may well be the most powerful educational force in this country today. It shapes our knowledge, attitudes, beliefs, and values. At the same time, its critics feel that in its present form television exerts its influence for the worst, that it misinforms and misdirects its audience, that figuratively speaking it drugs its viewers, leaving "its addicts waterlogged."

As you read to enjoy the following article by Nicholas Johnson, think about your own reactions to television. Is it the Great Educator or the Drug King?

WHAT DO WE DO ABOUT TELEVISION? by Nicholas Johnson

Television is more than just another great public resource—like air and water—ruined by private greed and public inattention. It is the greatest communications mechanism ever designed and operated by man. It pumps into the human brain an unending stream of information, opinion, moral values, and aesthetic taste. It cannot be a neutral influence. Every minute of television programming—commercials, entertainment, news—teaches us something.

Most Americans tell pollsters that television constitutes their principal source of information. Many of our senior citizens are tied to their television sets for intellectual stimulation. And children now spend more time learning from television than from church and school combined. By the time they enter first grade, they will have received more hours of instruction from television networks than they will later receive from college professors while earning a bachelor's degree. Whether they like it or not, the television networks are playing the roles of teacher, preacher, parent, public official, doctor, psychiatrist, family counselor, and friend for tens of millions of Americans each day of their lives.

TV programming can be creative, educational, uplifting, and refreshing without being tedious. But the current television product that drains away lifetimes of leisure energy is none of these. It leaves its addicts waterlogged. Only rarely does it contribute anything meaningful to their lives. No wonder so many Americans express to me a deep-seated hostility toward television. Too many realize, perhaps unconsciously but certainly with utter disgust, that television is itself a drug, constantly offering the allure of a satisfying fulfillment for otherwise empty and meaningless lives that it seldom, if ever, delivers. Well, what do we do about it?

Reader Response

Do you agree or disagree with Johnson? Do you think TV is harmful and dangerous, or do you think it has important benefits and merits? Or do you take a middle-of-the-road point of view—that there is both good and bad in television? In your response journal, write your thoughts. Remember that the journal gives you an informal writing opportunity to explore your feelings—to ask questions, raise issues, respond. You are, in essence, talking to yourself, so let your inner ear "listen." Explain your point of view. Give examples to support it.

Active Reading

In order to achieve emphasis, rhythm, and style, writers use a variety of sentence structures. Three main sentence parts—subject, predicate, and object—make up the body of every sentence. Study the Johnson article for its sentence variety. Lightly underline the simple subject(s), main verb(s), and object(s) in each sentence. What generalization can you make about Johnson's sentences?

Studying Model Writing Techniques

Sentence Variety Through Compound Subject, Predicate, and Object

REMEMBER! All sorts of choices are open to you in the kinds of words and sentences you use to express yourself.

All sentences have a subject as a main part. Subjects can be **simple,** consisting of a single word. Subjects can also be **compound,** consisting of two or more words.

SIMPLE SUBJECT:	Bolts *were in the drawer.*
COMPOUND SUBJECT:	Nuts *and* bolts *were in the drawer.*
COMPOUND SUBJECT:	Nuts, bolts, *and* screws *were in the drawer.*
COMPOUND SUBJECT:	Nuts, bolts, screws, staples, hinges, files, screwdrivers, hammers, pliers, *and* pieces of scrap metal *were in the drawer.*
SIMPLE SUBJECT:	*The* sofa *needed repairs.*
COMPOUND SUBJECT:	*The* sofa *and the* table *needed repairs.*
COMPOUND SUBJECT:	*The* sofa, *the* table, *and the* piano *needed repairs.*
COMPOUND SUBJECT:	*The* sofa, *the* table, *the* piano, *the* stool, *the* dresser, *the* beds, *and the* bookcase *needed repairs.*

Exercise 1   You can add variety and interest to your writing by using sentences with compound subjects. Form a single sentence with a compound subject from each of the following pairs of sentences. When necessary, make the appropriate change in the verb. The first one has been done for you as an example.

1. Work had left its mark on his face. Worry had left its mark on his face.

   Work and worry had left their marks on his face.

2. The young were mingled in the crowd. The old were mingled in the crowd.

   _____

3. The polar bear lives in the Arctic. The walrus lives in the Arctic.

   _____

4. Crabs thrive in the tidal pool. Sea urchins thrive in the tidal pool.

   _____

5. A ruler lay on the desk. A compass lay on the desk.

   _____

Exercise 2   Each of the following sentences has a simple subject. Revise each sentence so that it has a compound subject of at least three parts. The first is done for you as an example.

1. The mink coat had to be sold.

   The mink coat, the diamond necklace, the Rolls-Royce, and the silverware had to be sold.

2. Old newspapers cluttered the room.

   _____

   _____

3. Jogging can be a popular form of exercise.

   _____

   _____

4. Motorcycles jammed the streets.

   _____

   _____

5. Bologna may be displayed on the delicatessen counter.

   _____

   _____

6. Breads cost more.

   _____

   _____

7. Roses grew in the garden.

   _____

   _____

8. Earthquakes are natural disasters.

_____

_____

9. Shoes are made of leather.

_____

_____

10. Novels were studied in the course.

_____

_____

Subjects may be in the form of gerund phrases, infinitive phrases, or noun clauses, as well as single words. Look at the following examples of compound subjects.

GERUND PHRASES: Hiking across meadows, climbing hills, _and_ threading his way through forests _were his favorite pastimes in the spring._

INFINITIVE PHRASES: To see the wind fill the sail, to feel the salt spray, to fly noise-lessly over the ocean's surface _are among the joys of sailing._

NOUN CLAUSES: What he would find when he got home, what his wife would say to him, _and_ what explanation he could give to her _were the thoughts racing through his mind._

Exercise 3 Each of the following sentences has a simple subject in the form of a gerund phrase, infinitive phrase, or noun clause. Revise each sentence so that it has a compound subject by adding another gerund phrase, infinitive phrase, or noun clause. When necessary, make the appropriate change in the verb. The first has been done for you as an example.

1. Reading good books was the way she passed her days of convalescence. (Add another gerund phrase.) _Reading good books and listening to quiet music were the ways she passed_ _her days of convalescence._

2. Collecting stamps is his hobby. (Add another gerund phrase.)

_____

_____

3. Milking the cows is a farm chore. (Add another gerund phrase.)

_____

_____

4. To make long-distance phone calls adds to the cost of living. (Add another infinitive phrase.)

_____

_____

5. How we can curb inflation is a problem faced by the nation. (Add another noun clause.)

_____

_____

All sentences have a predicate verb as a second main part. Like subjects, predicates can be either simple or compound. Look at these examples.

SIMPLE PREDICATE: *The cat* awoke.
COMPOUND PREDICATE: *The cat* awoke *and* blinked.
COMPOUND PREDICATE: *The cat* awoke, blinked, *and* yawned.
COMPOUND PREDICATE: *The cat* awoke, blinked, yawned, *and* stretched.

SIMPLE PREDICATE: *Miranda* swims.
COMPOUND PREDICATE: *Miranda* swims *and* sings.
COMPOUND PREDICATE: *Miranda* swims, sings, dances, writes, cooks, *and* repairs *things around the house.*

Exercise 4   You can add variety and interest to your writing by using sentences with compound predicates. Form a single sentence with a compound predicate from each of the following pairs of sentences.

1. The embarrassed woman blushed. She departed.

_____

_____

2. He swung. He missed.

_____

3. The storm struck with a sudden fury. It destroyed houses.

_____

_____

4. The horse turned. It galloped toward home.

_____

5. The exhausted hiker rested against the wall of rock. He dozed in the warm sunshine.

_____

_____

Exercise 5   Each of the following sentences has a simple predicate. Revise each sentence so that it has a compound predicate of at least three parts. The first one has been done for you as an example.

1. The fighter reeled before the blow.

The fighter reeled before the blow, staggered backward, and fell to the canvas.

2. The oppressive heat dried the streams.

_____

_____

3. The driver blew his horn.

_____

_____

4. The young woman entered her office.

_____

_____

5. The cat crouched.

_____

_____

6. Meeting after such a long time, the two old friends greeted each other warmly.

_____

_____

7. A robin hopped across the lawn.

_____

_____

8. The crowd pushed forward.

_____

_____

9. After breakfast, she got behind the wheel.

_____

_____

10. The carpenter measured the wood.

_____

_____

Many, though not all, sentences have objects of the verb as a third main part. Like subjects and verbs, objects can be single or compound. Look at these examples.

SINGLE OBJECT: _He bought_ eggs.
COMPOUND OBJECT: _He bought_ eggs _and_ milk.
COMPOUND OBJECT: _He bought_ eggs, milk, _and_ cheese.
COMPOUND OBJECT: _He bought_ eggs, milk, cheese, bread, orange juice, ice cream, _and_ spaghetti.

SINGLE OBJECT:	*She wore a corduroy* jacket *of deep green.*
COMPOUND OBJECT:	*She wore a corduroy* jacket *of deep green and a yellow* sweater.
COMPOUND OBJECT:	*She wore a corduroy* jacket *of deep green, a yellow* sweater, *and a* pair *of worn blue jeans.*
COMPOUND OBJECT:	*She wore a corduroy* jacket *of deep green, a yellow* sweater, *a* pair *of worn blue jeans,* leather *gloves, and a* pair *of sunglasses.*

Objects may be in the form of gerund phrases, infinitive phrases, and noun clauses. Look at the following examples of compound objects.

GERUND PHRASES:	*The accusations included* driving recklessly, exceeding the speed limit, *and* crossing a double white line.
INFINITIVE PHRASES:	*The old fisherman told the boy* to bait his hook, to cast his line, *and* to wait patiently for a nibble.
NOUN CLAUSES:	*The driver asked* whether he should take the left or right fork *and* whether he could reach his destination before dark.

Exercise 6   You can add variety and interest to your writing by using sentences with compound objects. From each of the following pairs of sentences, form a single sentence with a compound object.

1. She had cereal. She had coffee.

_____

2. The lake had trout. The lake had bass.

_____

3. He enjoyed eating good food. He enjoyed drinking fine wine.

_____

4. The baby liked to play with his rattle. The baby liked to suck his thumb.

_____

_____

5. The lawyer insisted that her client had an ironclad alibi. The lawyer insisted that her client was innocent.

_____

_____

Exercise 7   Each of the following sentences has a single object, which is italicized. Revise each of the sentences so that it has a compound object of at least three parts. The first sentence is done for you as an example.

1. His pocket contained two *marbles.*

His pocket contained two marbles, a rusty nail, an old penny, and a rabbit's foot.

2. Into the refrigerator he put a *bottle of milk.*

_____

_____

3. Mary dusted the *table.*

_____

_____

4. The gardener planted *tomatoes.*

_____

_____

_____

5. Though no longer a child, he still believed *that there were elves in the woods.*

_____

_____

_____

6. The doctor ordered her *to get more sleep.*

_____

_____

_____

7. The soldiers disliked *going on long marches.*

_____

_____

_____

8. We learned from the newspapers *that two banks had been held up.*

_____

_____

_____

9. Into the trunk of the car she put *golf clubs.*

_____

_____

_____

10. From her apartment on the thirty-fourth floor, she could see *the river.*

_____

_____

Exercise 8 Now that you have had practice in writing and revising sentences with compound subjects, predicates, and objects, analyze the following sentences from "What Do We Do About Television?" by identifying the subject(s), predicate(s), and object(s). The first one has been done for you.

```
    subj.  pred.                               object
```
1. *It*   *pumps* into the human brain an unending *stream* of information, opinion, moral values, and aesthetic taste.

2. Most Americans tell pollsters that television constitutes their principal source of information.

3. By the time they enter first grade, they will have received more hours of instruction from television networks than they will later receive from college professors while earning a bachelor's degree.

4. Whether they like it or not, the television networks are playing the roles of teacher, preacher, parent, public official, doctor, psychiatrist, family counselor, and friend for tens of millions of Americans each day of their lives.

5. Too many realize, perhaps unconsciously but certainly with utter disgust, that television is itself a drug, constantly offering the allure of a satisfying fulfillment for otherwise empty and meaningless lives that it seldom, if ever, delivers.

RESPONSE

Modeling

Look at your journal entry. Of course, you wrote informally, so you were not thinking about sentence variety and all the fine points of good style. That's okay. But now look at your sentence structure. What revisions could you make that would increase sentence variety in your writing? Jot down some possible revisions.

COMPUTER HINT

If you did your journal entry at the keyboard, call up the file and make your revisions on the screen, but save the original for later reference. Thus, you will now have two files: your original informal journal entry and a set of sentences with which you have tried various revision techniques. You may even want to number the sentences, arrange them as if in an exercise (by using a hard return at the end of each sentence), and produce revisions immediately under each.

Writing

Now you are ready to write a critical essay on television programming. Although you may choose and develop your own subject, you may want to follow these suggestions:

Do you think TV is harmful and dangerous, or do you think it has important benefits and merits? Or do you take a middle-of-the-road point of view—that there is both good and bad in television? The composition you will write will state and explain your opinion regarding television.

If you are anti-television, you will probably want to devote the first paragraph to stating your general position. Here you can explain why you feel television is such a powerful influence, and you can state what you feel that influence is on the general audience. You can point out that its audience includes everyone from preschool children to our oldest citizens. You can point out how little effort it requires to watch pictures.

In the second and third paragraphs, you can give a few specific examples of programs, commercials, or TV personalities that you find objectionable. There are various ways you can organize these two paragraphs. You may wish to:

Devote one paragraph to programs and the other to commercials.
Devote one paragraph to programs for children and the other to programs for adults.
Devote one paragraph to one or two types of programs, such as sports and situation comedies, and the other to news broadcasts and interview shows.
Organize the middle section of your essay according to the ways in which television influences people. For example, you might devote one paragraph to how television affects the viewer's self-image and a second paragraph to how television affects the viewer's attitude toward others.
Organize these two paragraphs in some entirely different way.

In your final paragraph, you will probably want to make suggestions for improving the quality of TV broadcasting. Your suggestions may include some of the following, as well as others you will think of yourself: controlling the content and frequency of commercials; separating commercials from connection with any specific programs so that advertisers can no longer influence programs; cutting down the hours per week of TV broadcasting.

In writing the first draft of this composition, try to give conscious attention to two important aspects of organization: paragraph topic sentences and transition sentences that tie paragraphs together.

A good topic sentence states the main idea of the paragraph. Such a sentence helps you as the writer because it states just what you want to accomplish in the paragraph and helps you stick to your idea and make every word count. The topic sentence also helps your reader to follow your thinking easily. When the topic sentence is the first sentence in the paragraph, as it usually is, it also serves as an effective introduction or beginning.

To illustrate, here are two possible topic sentences for the first paragraph of your composition:

> *Brainwashing* is a dirty word to Americans, but, as we vegetate in front of the tube, we are happily submitting to as thorough a brainwashing as ever took place in the world.
> We have become a nation of videots.

Here are two possible topic sentences for the last paragraph:

> A few simple regulations can free us from the bondage of television as we know it.

> Just as we have made efforts to clean up the pollution of the land, water, and air, so we must take steps to clean up the pollution of our minds.

You have learned that thought must flow from one sentence to the next in a chain of meaning. Thought must also flow, in a similar way, from one paragraph to the next. Sometimes that flow is helped by transition sentences between paragraphs. A transition sentence can come at the end of a paragraph and prepare the reader for the following paragraph. A transition sentence can also come at the beginning of a paragraph, linking that paragraph to the preceding one. Here is an example of a transition sentence that might come at the end of paragraph one:

> Most of us readily recognize the deliberate lies and half-truths of commercials, but the equally damaging influence of the programs themselves is less obvious.

At the beginning of paragraph three, you might have a transition sentence such as the following:

> As we have seen, the police stories and the science fiction programs glorify violence and promote unrealistic attitudes.

If you are pro-television, you will probably want to devote the first paragraph to stating your general position. Here you may wish to state the general benefits and merits of television. You may wish to point out that television brings us the finest in entertainment and in sports; makes us world travelers; keeps us up to date on the news, on the latest in science and in health care; provides us with educational programs—all at little cost and little effort.

In your second and third paragraphs, you will want to give specific examples of the benefits and merits of television. These two paragraphs can be organized in various ways. Again, they can be broken up according to different types of programs. You may wish to devote one paragraph to entertainment programs and the other to educational programs, such as documentaries, news, and quiz shows. You may wish to devote one paragraph to specific types of people who benefit especially, such as the sick or housebound, children who would otherwise be bored, the poor who cannot afford more expensive forms of entertainment, the lonely who have little other human contact. You may wish to devote the other paragraph to examples of programs that are especially good for such people. Or you may wish to organize these two paragraphs in some entirely different way of your own choosing.

In your final paragraph, you may wish to view television as one of the benefits of science and technology. Like air and auto travel and air conditioning, TV adds to our comfort, happiness, and convenience. You may wish, instead, to conclude by discussing ways in which television broadcasting may become even better in the future or ways in which television might be put to better and wider use in the present. You may wish to conclude by discussing some one single program that you think is worthy and important and represents all the values of television. Or you may wish to conclude in some other way of your own preference.

If you take a middle-of-the-road position, you will probably want to devote your first paragraph to stating your general position. Succeeding paragraphs can be devoted, first, to an explanation of the merits and benefits of television, with specific examples and illustrations; second, to an explanation of the flaws and faults of television with specific examples and illustrations. In your concluding paragraph, you may wish to suggest ways in which television can be improved.

In writing the first draft of this composition, remember that you will try to give your conscious attention to two important aspects of organization: paragraph topic sentences and transition sentences that tie paragraphs together.

As you develop this first draft, concentrate on subject matter: your main ideas, explanations, and supporting examples. Later you will revise and polish.

COMPUTER HINT

Some of the sentences that you revised from your journal entry may now fit directly into your first draft. Provided your hardware and software have the capabilities, you can retrieve parts of that document, merge it into the draft document, and avoid retyping whole passages.

REVISION

Now that you have finished the first draft of your critical essay on television programming, you are ready to revise. In the revision process, we will focus on organization, chains of meaning, and proofreading details. Use the material as a model for your own revision process.

Checking Organization

Specific Examples for General Ideas

REMEMBER! Organized thinking is essential in composition writing.

An important skill of organization is the support of general ideas by specific examples. For instance, if you take the general idea "fragrant flowers," some examples you might give are *rose, peony, gardenia*. If you take the general idea "annoying insects," some examples you might give are *flies, mosquitoes, ants*.

Johnson does the same kind of thing when he refers to television networks playing *roles*. He takes that general idea and applies specifics: *teacher, preacher, parent, public official, doctor, psychiatrist, family counselor,* and *friend for tens of millions of Americans*. Likewise, he takes the general idea of television's being a *drug* and applies a specific description: *constantly offering the allure of a satisfying fulfillment for otherwise empty and meaningless lives that it seldom, if ever, delivers.*

These exercises will give you some practice in providing examples to support general ideas.

Exercise 9 Below you are given a general idea and one example. In the spaces provided, add two additional examples of your own.

1. Farm animals
   sheep   _____   _____

2. Wearing apparel
   shoes
   _____   _____

3. Careers
   electrician
   _____   _____

4. Household tools
   hammer
   _____   _____

5. Pollutants
   toxic chemical wastes
   _____   _____

6. Things seen in the sky
   lightning
   _____   _____

7. Great scientists
   Marie Curie
   _____   _____

8. Advantages of big-city living
   theaters
   _____   _____

9. Beautiful old buildings
   Notre Dame Cathedral
   _____   _____

10. Healthful foods
    fruit
    _____   _____

Exercise 10   Now you are given only the general idea. For each numbered item, supply three examples of your own.

1. Important rivers of the world

   _____   _____   _____

2. Enjoyable vacation activities

   _____   _____   _____

3. Natural fabrics

   _____   _____   _____

4. Common ailments

   _____   _____   _____

5. Boring chores

   _____   _____   _____

6. Circus performers

   _____   _____   _____

7. Things operated by a switch

   _____   _____   _____

8. Worthwhile hobbies

   _____   _____   _____

9. Current problem spots of the world

_____ _____ _____

10. Achievements of modern science and technology

_____ _____ _____

Modeling

Look at your first draft. Have you, like Johnson and the examples in the exercises above, included specific examples for general ideas? Study each of your sentences. Ask a peer editor to do likewise. When you find general ideas, add examples if they are missing.

Checking Chains of Meaning

Step-by-Step

REMEMBER! In composition writing, sentences are not individual or isolated. Instead, the thought is carried along from sentence to sentence in a chain of meaning.

Everything that happens or that you do takes place in a step-by-step order. A step-by-step account is a thought form that frequently shapes the chain of meaning in a sentence sequence. Johnson uses step-by-step organization in his second paragraph where he moves children to first grade, through college, to adulthood—all in front of the television set.

Exercise 11 Each of the following sentence sequences gives a step-by-step account. Following each example and using as few words as you can, make a list of the steps in each sequence. As a help, the first sequence is done for you.

1. The meal began with a cold antipasto of salami, peppers, chickpeas, anchovies, and provolone cheese. This was followed by a minestrone soup. The main dish was a delicious veal scallopine accompanied by spaghetti with olive oil and garlic sauce. Lemon ices and espresso capped off the splendid feast.

a. _Cold antipasto_ _____

b. _Minestrone soup_ _____

c. _Veal scallopine with spaghetti_ _____

d. _Lemon ices and espresso_ _____

2. At 5 A.M. the alarm I had set woke me. Still half-asleep, I showered quickly. I dressed suitably for the below-zero temperature that I knew awaited me outside. For breakfast, with the idea of having a warm interior as well as exterior, I had hot cereal, toast, and steaming tea. I donned my outer clothing. I stepped out into the bitter cold.

a. _____

b. _____

c. _____

d. _____

e. _____

f. _____

3. Knowing the test was to be crucial, she made it her business to study three hours a day during the preceding week. She sat down, finally, to the five-hour-long examination. During the next week, she waited for the results, able to think of nothing else. Finally, the results were posted. She had gotten an *A*. She rejoiced in her heart.

    a. _____

    b. _____

    c. _____

    d. _____

    e. _____

4. Turn on the power source for the computer. Then boot up the word-processing program. Enter the first draft at the keyboard, making only minimal corrections. Use revising and editing tools to make revisions. Print a copy, and save the final draft on disk for future reference.

    a. _____

    b. _____

    c. _____

    d. _____

    e. _____

    f. _____

5. Assemble all the papers you need, such as W-2 forms and records of deductible expenses. Read carefully the instructions that accompany the tax-return forms. Read the instructions a second time, even more carefully, checking each step against the tax-return form and your own papers. Using the extra form provided, prepare in pencil a first draft of your tax return. When this has been completed, double-check the arithmetic. From your penciled draft, copy in ink the final draft of your return.

    a. _____

    b. _____

    c. _____

    d. _____

    e. _____

    f. _____

Exercise 12   Now try writing two original step-by-step sequences. For your first sequence, write about an event, real or imaginary. An event means that some action is taken by you, another person, or a large number of people, or something happens to you, some other person, or a large number of people. Give the incidents of the event as they occur chronologically (in the order of their occurrence). Write three to six sentences.

_____

_____

_____

_____

_____

_____

_____

_____

For your second sequence, write about some recommended or customary action or procedure, such as how to spend Sundays, how to set up a tropical fish tank, how the heart works, how to start a car on a cold day, and so on. Give the steps in their natural or logical order. Write three to six sentences.

_____

_____

_____

_____

_____

_____

_____

_____

Modeling

If your critical essay on television programming includes a step-by-step process, make sure that you have the events in order and that your chains of meaning make the connections. If possible, ask a peer editor for his or her response.

Proofreading

As you proofread for errors in spelling and punctuation, you should also take note of the two common errors emphasized here for your attention: spelling and commonly confused words. The exercises that follow will help you to recognize and avoid these errors in your writing.

Spelling—The Terrible Twenty

Very few people can spell correctly twenty of the most frequently used words in the English language. In fact, those correct spellers belong to what may be the most exclusive club in the world. You are about to become a member! First, find out which words you need to learn.

Exercise 13   In the list below, you are given three possible spellings of ten of the words. Cross out the two incorrect spellings.

1. all right	alright	allright
2. changeable	changable	changible
3. seperation	seperetion	separation
4. skillful	skilfull	skillfull
5. occurance	occurrence	occurence
6. villian	villin	villain
7. embarass	embarrass	embarras
8. inoculate	innoculate	inocculate
9. occassionally	occasionally	ocassionally
10. desirable	desireable	desireble

Now turn to page 111 and carefully check your choices against the correct spellings. If you had them all right, you are halfway to membership in the club. If not, go to the next step.

Here are helpful hints for remembering the spelling of each of these words. Study the hints only for those words you got wrong. After studying the hint, cover the material with your hand. Close your eyes and picture the word, correctly spelled, in your mind. Then, keep the hint material covered and write the word correctly in the space provided. Review the spelling of any word you missed the first time by frequently challenging your friends or members of your family to spell it. If they get it wrong, tell them the right way.

1. *all right*
It's two words and two *l*'s. Think of *all wrong* and you'll have no trouble with *all right*.   _____

2. *changeable*
If a word ends in a silent *e* preceded by a soft *g* or a soft *c*, the *e* is not dropped when the suffix *-able* or *-ous* is added.

      change + -able = changeable
      courage + -ous = courageous
      notice + -able   = noticeable   _____

3. *separation*
Remember that it's "*par* for the course" for this word.   _____

4. *skillful*
This word is formed from the base *skill* and the suffix *-ful*.

      skill + -ful = skillful

Remember that the only word in the English language ending in *full* spelled with two *l*'s is the word *full* itself.

5. *occurrence*
Remember two *c*'s, two *r*'s, and *-ence* for this word.

occurr + -ence = occurrence

The rule that applies here is that if a word ends in a single consonant preceded by a single vowel and the accent is on the last syllable (or the word is of one syllable), then the final consonant is doubled when a suffix is added.

hop + -ed   = hopped
begin + -ing   = beginning
control + -ing = controlling

6. *villain*
This word comes from an older word meaning "a country person" or "a person who lived in the village" (as opposed to the nobles who lived in the castle). It may help you to remember that in *village* and *villain*, the second *l* is followed by an *a*.

7. *embarrass*
If you don't remember the two *r*'s and the two *s*'s for this word, your spelling may be embarrassing. Or you can contrast it with *harass*, which has only one *r*.

8. *inoculate*
Think of a needle. It looks like the number 1, and there's one of everything in *inoculate*.

9. *occasionally*
You just have to do the hard work of remembering the two *c*'s and the one *s*.

10. *desirable*
If a word ends in a silent *e*, the *e* is dropped when adding any suffix beginning with a vowel. (Remember that words in which the silent *e* is preceded by a soft *c* or *g* follow a different rule.)

desire + -able = desirable
hope + -ing   = hoping
come + -ing   = coming
store + -age   = storage

Exercise 14 Now you should be halfway to membership in the Terrible Twenty Club. Try going all the way with the next terrible ten. Cross out the wrong spellings.

1. privelege   priviledge   privilege

2. cematary   cemetery   cemetary

3. accomodate   acommodate   accommodate

4. sincerely   sincerly   sincerley

5. picnicing	picnicking	picknicking
6. benefitted	benefited	benifited
7. independanse	independance	independence
8. ecstacy	ecstesy	ecstasy
9. judgmant	judgment	judgement
10. supersede	supercede	superceed

Now turn to page 112 and carefully check your choices against the correct spelling. If you had them all right, congratulations on your membership! If not, go to the next step. Here are the helpful hints. Proceed as before.

1. *privilege*
For this word, there's no substitute for memorizing. The things to remember are that there are two *i*'s followed by two *e*'s and no *d* whatsoever.

_____

2. *cemetery*
Practically every other word you will use will end in *-ary*—*secretary, necessary, military, dictionary*. But with *cemetery* you come to the end of the *-ary* road! Remember there's a *meter* buried in ce*meter*y.

_____

3. *accommodate*
Just do the memory work. The word *accommodate* has two *c*'s and two *m*'s.

_____

4. *sincerely*
The silent *e* is retained when a suffix beginning with a consonant is added.

```
sincere + -ly      = sincerely
care + -ful         = careful
immediate + -ly = immediately
```

_____

5. *picnicking*
Words ending in *c* add a *k* when the suffixes *-e*, *-ing*, or *-y* are added.

```
picnic + -ing  = picnicking
picnic + -ed   = picnicked
panic + -y      = panicky
```

_____

6. *benefited*
If a word ends in a single consonant preceded by a single vowel and the accent is *not* on the last syllable, the final consonant remains single when a suffix is added.

```
benefit + -ed    = benefited
travel + -ing     = traveling
marvel + -ous   = marvelous
worship + -ing  = worshiping
```

_____

7. *independence*

The problem of *-ence* vs. *-ance* is a tough one in English spelling, and the only solution is pure memory persistence.

-ence	*-ance*
independence	attendance
excellence	performance
existence	reluctance
persistence	assistance

_____

8. *ecstasy*

Just remember that it's *s*, not *c* before the *y* in this word, and you'll be one of a very exclusive few!

_____

9. *judgment*

This word is the most important exception to the rules about silent *e*'s.

judge + -ment = judgment

Remember, no *e* with *g* in *judgment*.

_____

10. *supersede*

Remember this: Most words end with the *-cede* spelling, as in *accede, concede, precede, intercede, recede*. Three words end in *-ceed—succeed, exceed, proceed*. Only one word ends in *-sede—supersede*.

_____

Exercise 15 Now you should have full membership in the exclusive club of those who can spell the terrible twenty. To be sure, check yourself with a test on ten of them. Fill in the missing letter or letters, if needed.

1. ac_____om_____odate

2. picni_____ed

3. ecsta_____y

4. super_____ede

5. cemet_____ry

6. independ_____nce

7. priv_____lege

8. sep_____ration

9. i_____oculate

10. oc_____ur_____nce

COMPUTER HINT

A spell checker will help you catch certain common misspellings. Remember, however, that the spell checker simply recognizes incorrect spellings, not incorrect words. Avoid the false sense of security that a spell checker seems to afford some people. It is still necessary to check your paper carefully for correct spellings.

Commonly Confused Words

Now have a look at a troublesome ten. These are ten pairs of words that are not individually difficult to spell. However, they look alike and sound alike, so that people often spell one when they mean the other.

Exercise 16 Begin by testing yourself. Cross out the word that does not belong in each of the following sentences.

1. She was glad she did not (*lose, loose*) her purse because all her credit cards and her driver's license were in it.

2. She did not know (*weather, whether*) the purse would be returned.

3. Her passport was in her purse (*to, too*).

4. That purse was more expensive (*than, then*) her newer one.

5. At the time, she had (*quiet, quite*) a bit of money in her wallet.

6. A few hours (*past, passed*) before she received the welcome telephone call.

7. To write the thank-you note, she chose her best (*stationary, stationery*).

8. She wanted to show her appreciation with a small monetary reward, but the honest man would not (*accept, except*) it.

9. The (*affect, effect*) of the whole experience was to restore her faith in the human race.

10. She celebrated by treating herself to a luscious (*desert, dessert*) after dinner.

Study the following definitions and examples. Then evaluate your test results.

1. *loose—lose*
Loose means "not tight." To lose is the opposite of *to find*.

> After he lost weight, all his clothes were *loose*.
> Did Little Bo Peep *lose* her sheep?

2. *weather—whether*
Weather is rain, cold, wind, sun, and so on. *Whether* means "if."

> In September, the *weather* is usually lovely.
> They asked *whether* we would come to the party.

3. *to—too*
To is a preposition, as in "to the store," or part of an infinitive, as in "to run." *Too* means "also" or "very."

> She bowed *to* the applauding audience.
> I am *too* tired to go to the party.

4. *than—then*
Than is used in comparisons, as in "more expensive than." *Then* denotes time sequence: "First one thing happens, then another."

> Carlotta is taller *than* Martha.
> First, I will practice the piano, *then* eat lunch.

5. *quite—quiet*
Quite means "very." *Quiet* means "not noisy."

> That is *quite* a lot of money you have saved.
> The baby is *quiet* at last.

6. *past—passed*
As an adjective, *past* means "ended, just gone by, former." As a noun, *past* means "that which has become history" or "something that has happened." *Passed* is the past tense of *pass*, which means "to go, move along, proceed, succeed."

> She remembered her *past* trials and tribulations.
> Let us forget the *past* and begin all over.
> The parade *passed* up Fifth Avenue.

7. *stationary—stationery*
Stationary means "not moving." *Stationery* is paper.

> The dog sat *stationary*, just watching.
> He had new *stationery* printed when he moved.

8. *accept—except*
To *accept* means "to take or receive." *Except* is a preposition meaning "left out." To *except* is also a verb meaning "to leave out."

> Will you *accept* the job you have been offered?
> Everyone stood up *except* me.
> If we *except* the first paragraph, the contrast is satisfactory.

9. *affect—effect*
Affect is a verb and means "to influence." *Effect* as a noun means "result." The verb *to effect* means "to cause to happen."

> I was *affected* by the heat.
> The *effect* of the heat was felt by all.
> The doctor *effected* a remarkable cure.

10. *desert—dessert*
A *desert* is a hot, dry, barren place. A *dessert* is a goody at the end of a meal.

> They were lost in the *desert* and nearly perished.
> Her favorite *dessert* is rice pudding.

Answers to Exercise 13

1. all right		**6.** villain	
2. changeable		**7.** embarrass	
3. separation		**8.** inoculate	
4. skillful		**9.** occasionally	
5. occurrence		**10.** desirable	

1. privilege	**6.** benefited
2. cemetery	**7.** independence
3. accommodate	**8.** ecstasy
4. sincerely	**9.** judgment
5. picnicking	**10.** supersede

Modeling

After you have gone through the exercises, return to the literary model. Can you spot words in this essay that *could* have been confused? Did you notice any of the "terrible twenty"? Remember that spelling is, in large part, visual: we sometimes acknowledge that a written word "doesn't look right." Train your eye to pay attention to tricky words.

When you have completed the exercises and studied the model, give your composition a final proofreading.

Peer or Self-Evaluation Guidelines

Before you prepare a final copy of your critical essay on television programming, ask a peer or peers to read it and use the following guidelines for offering suggestions. Or use the guidelines as a means of self-evaluation.

	very well	*1*	*2*	*3*	*4*	*poorly*
1. How well does the essay illustrate a variety of sentence structures: compound subject, predicate, and object?						
2. How well does the writer include specific examples for general ideas?						
3. How well does the writer incorporate step-by-step sequences where necessary?						
4. How well has the writer avoided misspellings and the misuse of commonly confused words?						

The Final Draft: Sharing

Before you prepare your final draft for the publishing stage, take into consideration your peers' suggestions and/or your self-evaluation based on the guidelines. Add a title. Then read again to check for final details.

Unit 7

An Expository Essay About Crime

PREWRITING

Reading the Literature

Daily the news media will pour out the details of heinous crimes. Sensation creates bigger headlines and longer media time, but the close-to-home crimes affect us more personally. We all know someone whose wallet was stolen, whose house was burglarized, whose car was vandalized. Most of us know a victim of rape, stabbing, shooting, or assault.

As you read the following essay, written in 1968 by Robert K. Woetzel, remember that the statistics are now old, that crime has significantly increased since then, and that his warnings sound ominously familiar—and have obviously had no effect. And then think about how crime affects you. Personally. Daily.

CRIME AND VIOLENCE IN AMERICAN LIFE by Robert K. Woetzel

According to the uniform crime report released by the Federal Bureau of Investigation in June, 1968, there was a 17 percent increase in serious crime in the United States during the first three months of 1968, compared to the first three months of 1967. While the population of the nation has increased by 10 percent since 1960, crime has increased by 88 percent. The Senate Judiciary Committee has stated that "Crime is the most critical and urgent problem facing the nation," and Senator John L. McClellan of Arkansas has commented that "Crime and the threat of crime stalk America. Our streets are unsafe. Our citizens are fearful, terrorized, and outraged."

A recent survey in high-crime areas of two major cities showed that 43 percent of those interviewed stayed off the streets at night, 35 percent did not speak to strangers, 21 percent used only cabs and cars at night, and 20 percent wanted to move to another neighborhood because of fear. The federal government has authorized its employees doing overtime work to receive cab fare home because women employees are afraid to walk the streets of Washington after dark.

The FBI reports that crimes of violence climbed 18 percent during the first quarter of 1968, with murder up 16 percent; forcible rape, 19 percent; aggravated assault, 13 percent; and robbery, 24 percent. Armed robbery rose 26 percent, and aggravated assault with a firearm increased 23 percent. With more than twenty million citizens owning more than one hundred million firearms, about seventeen thousand gunshot deaths are reported every year.

Youth in ferment has been charged with a lion's share of crime: 75 percent of all arrests for major crimes are arrests of juveniles between the ages of eleven and twenty-four. Although racial minorities show a higher incidence of crime than does the more affluent white majority, increases of crime in affluent white suburbia have also been noted.

Crime and violence must be considered in the light of the American way of life. The bloodstained histories of Al Capone, "Lucky" Luciano, and other underworld figures are paralleled by the activities of America's frontier "heroes" like Jesse James and by moguls of the period of industrial expansion like Edward H. Harriman, who instigated the railroad wars in the state of New York. Movies have glorified many of these exploits. Violence is part of the daily fare of television programs and, indeed, has had a fascination for generations of Americans.

Reader Response

When we remember that Woetzel's article was written in the late 1960s, his statistics cause even more alarm. Check this year's almanac for current crime statistics (look in the index under "crime"), and then check last year's statistics for comparison. Finally, compare both to Woetzel's. In your response journal, make notes of the most telling statistics.

> ### COMPUTER HINT
> You may choose to include certain statistics in your upcoming essay. Keep in mind that you can create effective charts with most word-processing software. More sophisticated charts may require other software, but at least consider the option.

Next, in your journal, write informally in response to some or all of the following questions. To respond to all fully would be to write a book, so be selective and focus on what you think is most important and pertinent.

a. What personal experiences have you or people you know had with crime?

b. Why has crime worsened since 1968? What do you see as some of the major causes of the crime epidemic: softness on criminals? poverty and unemployment? racism and prejudice? drugs? violence in sporting events both among players and fans? violence in TV, video games, and movies? wars? inflation? pollution of the environment? greed, cynicism, and corruption among some government and business leaders? loss of national confidence and idealism? the breakdown of the family? a decreasing influence of religion?

c. Do you feel that there is no new crime epidemic at all? that it is part of human nature to be violent and thoughtless? that there always has been and always will be violent crime, with only the forms changing? or that the extent of crime is always about the same, but nowadays we care about it more?

d. How can crime be controlled or reduced? What steps would you like to see taken in your local community? in your state? in the national policy?

Active Reading

Reread "Crime and Violence in American Life" and take note of Woetzel's sentence structure. Notice particularly what kinds of modifiers he uses and how they work. Underline lightly the modifying structures that you spot readily.

Studying Model Writing Techniques

Sentence Variety with Compound Modifiers

REMEMBER! All sorts of choices are open to you in the kinds of words and sentences you use to express yourself.

You know that the two main parts of all sentences are the subject and the verb. You also know that many sentences include an object of the verb as the third main part. As you have learned, these three sentence parts can be compounded for sentence variety.

In addition, many sentences have modifiers, which can also be compound. Study these examples.

Single-Word Adjectives

SINGLE: *I saw before me a* **strange** *room.*
COMPOUND: *I saw before me a* **strange, untidy, cluttered, fascinating** *room.*

Adjective Prepositional Phrases

SINGLE: *Lincoln advocated government* of the people.
COMPOUND: *Lincoln advocated government* of the people, by the people, and for the people.

Participial Phrases

SINGLE: Screaming curses, *the mob surged forward.*
COMPOUND: Screaming curses, waving sticks and banners, hurling rocks, *the mob surged forward.*

Adjective Clauses

SINGLE: *No one* who has a grain of common sense *will agree with the committee's plan.*
COMPOUND: *No one* who has a grain of common sense, who has given any thought to the problem, who cares about the future *will agree with the committee's plan.*

Words in Apposition

SINGLE: *Ben Franklin, statesman, was a Great American.*

COMPOUND: *Ben Franklin, statesman, scientist, philosopher, and* journalist, *was a great American.*

Single-Word Adverbs

SINGLE: *He pleaded* earnestly, *but she would not listen.*

COMPOUND: *He pleaded* earnestly, softly, hastily, pitifully, *but she would not listen.*

Adverb Prepositional Phrases

SINGLE: *The crew rowed* in perfect rhythm.

COMPOUND: *The crew rowed* in perfect rhythm, with sweeping power, through still water and rough.

Adverb Clauses

SINGLE: Because he had known one defeat too many, *he finally gave up the struggle.*

COMPOUND: Because he had known one defeat too many *and* because he had lost all hope, *he finally gave up the struggle.*

Exercise 1 Identify the italicized modifier in each of these sentences from the literary selection on pages 113-114. The first one is done for you.

1. There was a 17 percent increase in serious crime in the United States *during the first three months of 1968.*

   adverb prepositional phrase

2. *While the population of the nation has increased by 10 percent since 1960,* crime has increased by 88 percent.

   _____

3. Our citizens are *fearful, terrorized, and outraged.*

   _____

4. The federal government has authorized its employees *doing overtime work* to receive cab fare home.

   _____

5. The federal government has authorized its employees doing overtime work to receive cab fare home *because women employees are afraid to walk the streets of Washington after dark.*

   _____

Exercise 2 Each of the following sentences has a single modifier in italics. Revise each sentence by adding at least one additional modifier. Be sure that the modifiers you add are of the same kind as the one already given. The first four are done for you as examples.

116

1. It was a house *of weathered pine.*

   It was a house of weathered pine, without windows, of primitive construction.

2. The building collapsed *suddenly.*

   The building collapsed suddenly, explosively, destructively.

3. A dog like Buck, *who had been pampered and petted,* could not understand this new harsh environment.

   A dog like Buck, who had been pampered and petted, who had never known an unkind word or gesture could not understand this new harsh environment.

4. *Smiling warmly,* the woman approached the frightened child.

   Smiling warmly and extending her hands, the woman approached the frightened child.

5. His *gaunt* face bespoke a hard life at sea.

6. *When the sun set,* peace and quiet settled over the land.

7. He tried to ride the bicycle, *which was too big for him.*

8. *Groaning in pain,* the injured man called for help.

9. The acrobat went through her routine *with skill.*

10. The bee, *pollinator of flowers,* is among our insect friends.

11. The tidal wave ripped *over the beach.*

12. *Heaving a sigh of relief,* she sat on the couch.

RESPONSE

Modeling

Return to your journal entry in which you explored your feelings about crime. Although you wrote informally without concern for sentence structure and style, read through your entry looking for modifiers. Did you use mostly single-word modifiers and prepositional phrases? Do you see sentences that could be improved, like those in the exercise above, by creating compound modifiers? Make notes to yourself or jot down revisions that improve the sentences and your meaning.

Writing

Using the reader response ideas generated by reading Woetzel's article, begin your first draft of an expository essay about crime. Although you may choose and develop your own topic, you may wish to follow these suggestions:

First, be selective and focus on what you think is most important and pertinent. For instance, in your first paragraph you may wish to give a precise, vivid account of one crime you know about personally or have learned about from the newspaper or TV. You would conclude this paragraph with two sentences. The first would suggest that this one example is representative of a general condition. For instance, suppose the victims of the crime you discussed were Mr. and Mrs. Smith. You might write: "Each and every day a thousand Mr. and Mrs. Smiths are mugged and beaten." The second, a transition sentence, might lead into your discussion in the next two paragraphs of what you consider the two major causes of widespread crime. An example of such a sentence is the very simple question, "Why?"

The second and third paragraphs might each be devoted to a thorough discussion of what you believe to be two important causes of widespread crime. In discussing these causes, try to be objective, clear, and logical—not emotional and rhetorical. Try to avoid sweeping and meaningless generalizations. For example, it is useless to say, "What we need is more law and order." We have plenty of law; getting order, or obedience to the law, is the problem, not the solution. Simplistic discussions of softness on criminals and the need for capital punishment probably are irrelevant because capital punishment would apply to one case in millions. Moreover, in the "good old days" when heads were chopped off right and left, there were plenty of murders, or else heads would not have been chopped off right and left.

You may wish to devote your fourth and concluding paragraph to a few recommendations you would care to make to help solve the problem. Or you may wish to take an entirely different tack and state what precautions you and others can take to minimize the personal risk of exposure to crime. As a third possibility, you may wish to have a change of tone, and end your composition on a satirical or imaginative note. For instance, you may wish for a return to the romantic days of long ago when criminals had glamour and appeal, like Robin Hood, The Highwayman, Captain Kidd, and Jesse James.

As you develop your first draft, concentrate on subject matter: your main ideas and supporting explanations. Later you will revise and proofread.

REVISION

Now that you have finished the first draft of your expository essay about crime, you are ready to revise. In the revision process, we will focus on organization, chains of meaning, and proofreading details. Use the materials as a model for your own revision process.

Checking Organization

General Ideas for Specific Examples

REMEMBER! Organized thinking is essential in composition writing.

An important skill of organization is the ability to recognize and provide the **general ideas** that are suggested by **specific examples.** The exercise that follows will give you some practice in that skill.

In the previous unit, you thought about examples of general ideas. Now you will reverse that process. You will be given several examples and will be asked to recognize a general idea that they represent. For instance, if you are given the examples *cars, bicycles, trucks,* and *buses,* you can recognize that they illustrate the general idea "vehicles." If you are given the examples *swimming, jogging, skiing,* and *golf,* you can recognize that they illustrate the general idea "sports activities for one person." If you are given the examples *saber-toothed tiger, pterodactyl, dinosaur,* and *mastodon,* you can recognize that they illustrate the general idea "prehistoric animals."

Exercise 3 In the following sentences from Woetzel's article, what general idea does each of these groups of specifics suggest? The first is done for you.

1. A recent survey showed that 43 percent . . . stayed off the streets at night, 35 percent did not speak to strangers, 21 percent used only cabs and cars at night. . . .

   between one-fifth and two-fifths feel threatened

2. While the population of the nation has increased by 10 percent since 1960, crime has increased by 88 percent.

   _____

3. Crimes of violence climbed 18 percent . . . with murder up 16 percent; forcible rape, 19 percent; aggravated assault, 13 percent; and robbery, 24 percent.

   _____

4. The bloodstained histories of Al Capone, "Lucky" Luciano, and other underworld figures are paralleled . . .

   _____

5. . . . paralleled by the activities of America's frontier "heroes" like Jesse James and by moguls of the period of industrial expansion like Edward H. Harriman.

   _____

Exercise 4 Look at each group of examples. In your own words, write in the space provided the general idea represented by each group of examples. The first one has been done for you as an example.

1. cheddar, Roquefort, Swiss, cottage

   cheese

2. bicycles, roller skates, skateboards, ice skates

   _____

3. lipstick, powder, rouge, eyeliner

   _____

4. Susan B. Anthony, Eleanor Roosevelt, Harriet Tubman, Emily Dickinson

5. magnetism, heat, light, electricity

6. volcanoes, earthquakes, floods, hurricanes

7. housing, food, clothing, employment

8. triangle, square, rectangle, circle

9. smallpox, bubonic plague, polio, diphtheria

10. button, zipper, hook and eye, clasp

11. sailboats, gliders, weather vanes, kites

12. spears, crossbows, swords, catapults

13. contracts, wills, leases, deeds

14. Alexander, Napoleon, Caesar, Hitler

15. broken glass, empty cans, paper, cigarette butts

Modeling

Reread your first draft and study the organization details. Do your specific examples lead readers clearly to the general idea? Or do you leave them guessing about what you are trying to say? If possible, ask a peer editor to help you respond to these questions. Revise as necessary.

Checking Chains of Meaning

Generalizations and Examples

REMEMBER! In composition writing, sentences are not individual or isolated. Instead, the thought is carried along from sentence to sentence in a chain of meaning.

Some statements are broad and general. They are called **generalizations.** Study the following generalizations from the literary selection at the beginning of this unit:

_____ **1.** Youth in ferment has been charged with a lion's share of crime.

_____ **2.** Our citizens are fearful, terrorized, and outraged.

_____ **3.** Crime and violence must be considered in the light of the American way of life.

Some statements give **specific examples.** The following are statements of specific examples, also from the literary selection at the beginning of this unit. They support the generalizations above.

a. Seventy-five percent of all arrests for major crimes are arrests of juveniles between the ages of eleven and twenty-four.

b. A recent survey . . . showed that 43 percent . . . stayed off the streets at night, 35 percent did not speak to strangers, 21 percent used only cabs and cars at night, and 20 percent wanted to move to another neighborhood because of fear. The federal government has authorized its employees doing overtime work to receive cab fare home because women employees are afraid to walk the streets of Washington after dark.

c. The bloodstained histories of Al Capone, "Lucky" Luciano, and others . . . are paralleled by the activities of America's frontier "heroes" like Jesse James and by moguls . . . like Edward H. Harriman. . . . Movies have glorified many of the exploits. Violence is part of the daily fare of television programs and, indeed, has had a fascination for generations of Americans.

Exercise 5 Each of the three generalizations you have looked at (1 to 3) goes with one of the three statements of examples (*a* to *c*). Match them to create a sentence sequence. In the space provided alongside each generalization, write the letter of the matching statements of examples.

Exercise 6 Now try your hand at writing your own generalizations. In the space provided, write a good general statement to form a sentence sequence with the given statement of examples.

1. _____

The bee gives us honey and, along with the butterfly, pollinates flowers. The praying mantis destroys harmful bugs.

2. _____

_____

We love French fries and egg foo yong. We devour yogurt and chili con carne. Spaghetti and pizza are among our great delicacies.

3. _____

_____

The horse is a prime example. The ox, the donkey, the camel, and the elephant have done their share as well.

4. _____

_____

Among these are earthquakes, volcanic eruptions, floods, and hurricanes.

5. _____

_____

Dishes have to be washed. Laundry has to be done. Garbage has to be taken out. Furniture has to be dusted.

6. _____

_____

We have gone to the polar ice caps. We have gone to the peak of Everest and to the ocean floor. We have gone to the moon.

7. _____

_____

The dictionary is indispensable. A good encyclopedia is frequently useful. The thesaurus can be helpful.

8. _____

_____

"Satchel" Paige, who was a major league pitcher in his 60s, is a case in point. Arnold Palmer, a golf champion in middle age, is another.

9. _____

_____

The Eskimos have survived the Arctic north, the Berbers the desert waste, the Amazon Indians the tropical jungle.

10. _____

_____

More advanced solar energy can be developed. We can learn to harness the tides and the wind. Someday we will tap the great forces of gravity and earth's magnetism.

Exercise 7   Now try the reverse. Each of the following statements is a generalization. Form a sentence sequence by adding statements of appropriate examples. You can add one, two, or three sentences to form each sequence.

1. Some TV "personalities" are obnoxious.

_____

_____

2. Autumn has great pleasures to offer.

_____

_____

_____

_____

3. Some musical instruments are played by the use of the hands only.

_____

_____

_____

_____

4. There are several ways to get about by the use of "leg power."

_____

_____

_____

_____

5. Trees are useful to us in many ways.

_____

_____

_____

_____

6. Being a teenager these days is more difficult than it was in the past.

_____

_____

_____

7. Certain colors go together particularly well.

_____

_____

_____

8. We are deeply dependent on "public servants."

_____

_____

_____

_____

9. Today, women are working in jobs that were once "for men only."

_____

_____

_____

_____

10. The best things in life are free.

_____

_____

_____

_____

Modeling

As you make further revisions on your expository essay draft, take note of the generalizations and examples you have included. Do your examples resemble those in the Woetzel essay? Remember that to include generalizations without examples is to leave your reader guessing about your meaning.

Since the necessity of examples for every generalization may be the most difficult stumbling block for writers, give this section your careful attention. Ask a peer or peers for their response as well. Then revise as necessary.

> ### COMPUTER HINT
> Use your word-processing software to help you check for unsupported generalizations. Identify generalizations with bold type. Then make sure that adequate examples follow—or lead up to—the bold-typed sentences.

Proofreading

As you proofread for errors in spelling and punctuation, take note of two common errors emphasized for your attention: case of personal pronouns and the use of *who, whom,* and *whose.* The exercises that follow will help you to recognize and avoid these errors in your writing.

Personal Pronouns—Case

Except for the possessive case, most nouns and pronouns do not change their form regardless of how they are used in a sentence. The personal pronouns are an exception. *I, we, he, she,* and *they* change their form to *me, us, him, her,* and *them* when these words are used as the object of a verb, the object of a preposition, or an indirect object. First, look over the table below; then study the examples that follow.

Nominative Forms	Objective Forms
Use as subjects and as predicate nominatives.	*Use as direct objects, indirect objects, and objects of prepositions.*
I	me
he, she, it	him, her, it
you	you
we	us
they	them
you	you

WRONG: *Him and me are going.*
RIGHT: *He and I are going.*
REASON: *He and I are the compound subject of the sentence. The objective case,* him *and* me, *cannot be used for the subject.*

WRONG: *Between you and I, that horse is going to win the race.*
RIGHT: *Between you and me, that horse is going to win the race.*
REASON: *The personal pronouns are objects of the preposition* between. *Therefore, the objective case form—*me*—must be used.* You *is in the objective case as well, but since its form doesn't change with case,* you *is no problem.*

WRONG: *The one who is to blame is me.*
RIGHT: *The one who is to blame is* I.
REASON: *The linking verb* is *does not take an object. The personal pronoun in this sentence is a predicate nominative. Therefore, the nominative form* I *must be used.*

WRONG: *He called my sister and I.*
RIGHT: *He called my sister and* me.
REASON: *The pronoun is the object of the verb* called. *The objective case,* me, *must be used.*

WRONG: *Lawrence studies harder than me.*
RIGHT: *Lawrence studies harder than* I.
REASON: *The personal pronoun is the subject of the understood verb* do *in the clause "than I (do)."*

When you are writing or speaking about yourself and another person or persons, it is customary to mention yourself last.

WRONG: *I and my brother took our parents out to dinner.*
RIGHT: *My brother and I took our parents out to dinner.*

Exercise 8   Eight of the following sentences contain a personal pronoun in the wrong case. Rewrite the sentence, correcting the error. Leave the two correct sentences alone.

1. Just between you and me, my mother was right.

_____

_____

2. Kirsten likes to swim as much as me.

_____

3. When me and my sister got off the train, there was nobody to meet us.

_____

_____

4. I am older than her.

_____

5. Susan and she turned back.

_____

6. Us girls are all going to the dance next week.

_____

7. He speaks Spanish better than me.

_____

8. She asked Jack and I to help her fix the flat.

_____

9. Few of my friends work as hard as me.

_____

10. European countries welcome we Americans as tourists.

_____

_____

Using Who, Whom, Whose

The pronoun _who_ can be as troublesome as the personal pronouns because it has its own special case forms: _who_ for the nominative, _whom_ for the objective, and _whose_ for the possessive. The word _who's_ is always a contraction for _who is_, never the possessive. Look at the table and the examples.

Nominative Case	Objective Case	Possessive Case
Use as subject and predicate nominative.	_Use as direct object, indirect object, and object of preposition._	_Use to show possession._
who	whom	whose
whoever	whomever	

WRONG:	_Cast your vote for whomever promises to lower taxes._
RIGHT:	_Cast your vote for_ whoever _promises to lower taxes._
REASON:	_The pronoun_ whoever _is the subject of the verb_ promises.

WRONG:	_The man who I will marry just walked in the door._
RIGHT:	_The man_ whom _I will marry just walked in the door._
REASON:	_The pronoun_ whom _is the object of the verb_ will marry. (_I will marry him._)

WRONG:	_This is the man who we chose as the winner._
RIGHT:	_This is the man_ whom _we chose as the winner._
REASON:	_The pronoun_ whom _is the object of the verb_ chose.

How much progress are you making? The reason for using either *who* or *whom* is omitted from the next three examples. You supply the reasons.

WRONG: *Whom is the best dressed person in the room?*
RIGHT: Who *is the best dressed person in the room?*

REASON: _____

   _____

WRONG: *Who will the people elect in November?*
RIGHT: Whom *will the people elect in November?*

REASON: _____

   _____

WRONG: *To who did you send the invitation?*
RIGHT: To whom *did you send the invitation?*

REASON: _____

   _____

WRONG: *The woman who's bike I borrowed wants it back.*
RIGHT: *The woman* whose *bike I borrowed wants it back.*
REASON: *The sentence calls for the possessive* whose, *showing ownership of the bike.*

WRONG: *The woman whose the owner of the bike wants it back.*
RIGHT: *The woman* who's *the owner of the bike wants it back.*
REASON: *The sentence calls for* who's, *the contraction of* who is.

The reason for using *whose* or *who's* is omitted from the remaining examples. You supply the reasons.

WRONG: *Who's life is it anyway?*
RIGHT: Whose *life is it anyway?*

REASON: _____

   _____

WRONG: *Whose going to the movie with me?*
RIGHT: Who's *going to the movie with me?*

REASON: _____

   _____

Exercise 9   Each of the following sentences makes use of the pronoun *who* or one of its forms: *whom, whose, who's.* Six of the sentences contain an error in the form of the pronoun. Four are correct. Rewrite the incorrect sentences to eliminate the error. Leave the others alone.

1. To whom did you address the package I gave you to mail?

_____

_____

_____

2. She is a woman who I have admired all my life.

3. The eagle, who's wings were still spread wide, had just alighted on the perch.

4. The most popular performer was the clown, whom the audience had been applauding all afternoon.

5. Whom, in your opinion, is the best performer?

6. The troops, who's long hike had exhausted them, stopped for a rest.

7. The tenants to who the landlord had sent the notice were furious.

8. The fire fighter who is climbing the ladder is in great danger.

9. Give the thermometer to the nurse who's on duty.

10. The only one who the college selected for admission had been a mediocre student in high school.

Modeling

After you have gone through the exercises, return to the literary model. Notice Woetzel's use of pronouns. Can you identify the case of each? Consider these model sentences:

a. *Our* streets are unsafe. (possessive case)

b. The federal government has authorized *its* employees doing overtime work to receive cab fare home. . . . (possessive case)

c. The bloodstained histories of . . . underworld figures are paralleled by the activities of America's frontier "heroes" like . . . Edward H. Harriman, *who* instigated the railroad wars. . . . (nominative case)

When you have finished the exercises and studied the model, give your composition a final proofreading.

Peer or Self-Evaluation Guidelines

Before you prepare a final copy of your expository essay about crime, ask a peer or peers to read it and use the following guidelines for offering suggestions. Or use the guidelines as a means of self-evaluation.

	very well	*1*	*2*	*3*	*4*	*poorly*
1. How well does the expository essay include a variety of modifiers?						
2. How well does the expository essay include compound modifiers?						
3. How well does the writer use specific examples to imply general ideas?						
4. How well does the writer use examples to support his/her generalizations?						
5. How well does the writer use the accurate cases of personal and relative pronouns, including *who, whom,* and *whose*?						

The Final Draft: Sharing

Before you prepare your final draft for the publishing stage, take into consideration your peers' suggestions and/or your self-evaluation based on the guidelines above. Add a title. Then read again to check for final details.

COMPUTER HINT

Use the formatting commands in your word-processing software to create an attractive final copy. Center the title. Create a running header or footer, either with your name and page number or with the title and page number. (Ask your instructor if he/she has a preference.) You may also choose (with your instructor's approval) to justify the right margins or alter the type size for the title.

Unit 8

An Imaginative Personal Essay About Winning a Lottery

PREWRITING

Reading the Literature

With many states promoting lotteries and with regular media coverage of the handful who win millions in those games of chance, many of us have probably tried to imagine what it would be like to be lottery winners. We imagine how our lives would change or what we would do with the money—quit working, travel, buy luxuries; donate to charities, help the homeless, finance medical research; win friends, influence politicians, gain fame. The list is as long as the odds.

As you read to enjoy the following short story by Russian author Anton Chekhov, try to imagine how you would feel as Ivan or his wife Masha.

THE LOTTERY TICKET by Anton Chekhov

Ivan Dmitritch, a middle-class man who lived with his family on an income of twelve hundred a year and was very well satisfied with his lot, sat down on the sofa after supper and began reading the newspaper.

"I forgot to look at the newspaper today," his wife said to him as she cleared the table. "Look and see whether the list of drawings is there."

"Yes, it is," said Ivan Dmitritch; "but hasn't your ticket lapsed?"

"No; I took the interest on Tuesday."

"What is the number?"

"Series 9,499, number 26."

"All right . . . we will look . . . 9,499 and 26."

Ivan Dmitritch had no faith in lottery luck, and would not, as a rule, have consented to look at the lists of winning numbers, but now, as he had nothing else to do and as the newspaper was before his eyes, he passed his finger downward along the column of numbers. And immediately, as though in mockery of his skepticism, no further than the second line from the top, his eye was caught by the figure 9,499! Unable to believe his eyes, he hurriedly dropped the paper on his knees without looking to see the number of the ticket and, just as though someone had given him a douche of cold water, he felt an agreeable chill in the pit of the stomach; tingling and terrible and sweet!

"Masha, 9,499 is there!" he said in a hollow voice.

His wife looked at his astonished and panic-stricken face, and realized that he was not joking.

"9,499?" she asked, turning pale and dropping the folded tablecloth on the table.

"Yes, yes . . . it really is there!"

"And the number of the ticket?"

"Oh, yes! There's the number of the ticket too. But stay . . . wait! No, I say! Anyway, the number of our series is there! Anyway, you understand. . . ."

Looking at his wife, Ivan Dmitritch gave a broad, senseless smile, like a baby when a bright object is shown it. His wife smiled too; it was as pleasant to her as to him that he only mentioned the series and did not try to find out the number of the winning ticket. To torment and tantalize oneself with hopes of possible fortune is so sweet, so thrilling!

"It is our series," said Ivan Dmitritch, after a long silence. "So there is a probability that we have won. It's only a probability, but there it is!"

"Well, now look!"

"Wait a little. We have plenty of time to be disappointed. It's on the second line from the top, so the prize is seventy-five thousand. That's not money, but power, capital! And in a minute I shall look at the list, and there—26! Eh? I say, what if we really have won?"

The husband and wife began laughing and staring at one another in silence. The possibility of winning bewildered them; they could not have said, could not have dreamed, what they both needed that seventy-five thousand for, what they would buy, where they would go. They thought only of the figures 9,499 and 75,000 and pictured them in their imagination, while somehow they could not think of the happiness itself which was so possible.

Ivan Dmitritch, holding the paper in his hand, walked several times from corner to corner, and only when he had recovered from the first impression began dreaming a little.

"And if we have won," he said—"why, it will be a new life, it will be a transformation! The ticket is yours, but if it were mine I should, first of all, of course, spend twenty-five thousand on real property in the shape of an estate; ten thousand on immediate expenses, new furnishing . . . traveling . . . paying debts, and so on. . . . The other forty thousand I would put in the bank and get interest on it."

"Yes, an estate, that would be nice," said his wife, sitting down and dropping her hands in her lap.

"Somewhere in the Tula or Oryol provinces. . . . In the first place we shouldn't need a summer villa, and besides, it would always bring in an income."

And pictures came crowding on his imagination, each more gracious and poetical than the last. And in all these pictures he saw himself well-fed, serene, healthy, felt warm, even hot! Here, after eating a summer soup, cold as ice, he lay on his back on the burning sand close to a stream or in the garden under a lime tree.... It is hot.... His little boy and girl are crawling about near him, digging in the sand or catching ladybirds in the grass. He dozes sweetly, thinking of nothing, and feeling all over that he need not go to the office today, tomorrow, or the day after. Or, tired of lying still, he goes to the hayfield, or to the forest for mushrooms, or watches the peasants catching fish with a net. When the sun sets he takes a towel and soap and saunters to the bathing-shed, where he undresses at his leisure, slowly rubs his bare chest with his hands, and goes into the water. And in the water, near the opaque soapy circles, little fish flit to and fro and green water-weeds nod their heads. After bathing there is tea with cream and milk rolls.... In the evening a walk or *vint* with the neighbors.

"Yes, it would be nice to buy an estate," said his wife, also dreaming, and from her face it was evident that she was enchanted by her thoughts.

Ivan Dmitritch pictured to himself autumn with its rains, its cold evenings, and its St. Martin's summer.* At that season he would have to take longer walks about the garden and beside the river, so as to get thoroughly chilled, and then drink a big glass of vodka and eat a salted mushroom or a soused cucumber, and then—drink another.... The children would come running from the kitchen garden, bringing a carrot and a radish smelling of fresh earth.... And then, he would lie stretched full length on the sofa, and in leisurely fashion turn over the pages of some illustrated magazine, or, covering his face with it and unbuttoning his waistcoat, give himself up to slumber.

The St. Martin's summer is followed by cloudy, gloomy weather. It rains day and night, the bare trees weep, the wind is damp and cold. The dogs, the horses, the fowls—all are wet, depressed, downcast. There is nowhere to walk; one can't go out for days together; one has to pace up and down the room, looking despondently at the gray window. It is dreary!

Ivan Dmitritch stopped and looked at his wife.

"I should go abroad, you know, Masha," he said.

And he began thinking how nice it would be in late autumn to go abroad somewhere to the South of France ... to Italy ... to India!

"I should certainly go abroad too," his wife said. "But look at the number of the ticket!"

"Wait, wait!"

He walked about the room and went on thinking. It occurred to him: what if his wife really did go abroad? It is pleasant to travel alone, or in the society of light, careless women who live in the present, and not such as think and talk all the journey about nothing but their children, sigh, and tremble with dismay over every farthing. Ivan Dmitritch imagined his wife in the train with a multitude of parcels, baskets, and bags; she would be sighing over something, complaining that the train made her head ache, that she had spent so much money.... At the stations he would continually be having to run for boiling water, bread and butter.... She wouldn't have dinner because of its being too dear....

* *St. Martin's summer* Indian summer, in November

132

"She would begrudge me every farthing," he thought, with a glance at his wife. "The lottery ticket is hers, not mine! Besides, what is the use of her going abroad? What does she want there? She would shut herself up in the hotel, and not let me out of her sight.... I know!"

And for the first time in his life his mind dwelt on the fact that his wife had grown elderly and plain, and that she was saturated through and through with the smell of cooking, while he was still young, fresh, and healthy, and might well have got married again.

"Of course, all that is silly nonsense," he thought; "but ... why should she go abroad? What would she make of it? And yet she would go, of course.... I can fancy.... In reality it is all one to her, whether it is Naples or Klin. She would only be in my way. I should be dependent upon her. I can fancy how, like a regular woman, she will lock the money up as soon as she gets it.... She will hide it from me.... She will look after her relations and grudge me every farthing."

Ivan Dmitritch thought of her relations. All those wretched brothers and sisters and aunts and uncles would come crawling about as soon as they heard of the winning ticket, would begin whining like beggars, and fawning upon them with oily, hypocritical smiles. Wretched, detestable people! If they were given anything, they would ask for more; while if they were refused, they would swear at them, slander them, and wish them every kind of misfortune.

Ivan Dmitritch remembered his own relations, and their faces, at which he had looked impartially in the past, struck him now as repulsive and hateful.

"They are such reptiles!" he thought.

And his wife's face, too, struck him as repulsive and hateful. Anger surged up in his heart against her, and he thought malignantly:

"She knows nothing about money, and so she is stingy. If she won it she would give me a hundred roubles, and put the rest away under lock and key."

And he looked at his wife, not with a smile now, but with hatred. She glanced at him too, and also with hatred and anger. She had her own daydreams, her own plans, her own reflections; she understood perfectly well what her husband's dreams were. She knew who would be the first to try and grab her winnings.

"It's very nice making daydreams at other people's expense!" is what her eyes expressed. "No, don't you dare!"

Her husband understood her look; hatred began stirring again in his breast, and in order to annoy his wife he glanced quickly, to spite her at the fourth page on the newspaper and read out triumphantly:

"Series 9,499, number 46! Not 26!"

Hatred and hope both disappeared at once, and it began immediately to seem to Ivan Dmitritch and his wife that their rooms were dark and small and low-pitched, that the supper they had been eating was not doing them good, but lying heavy on their stomachs, that the evenings were long and wearisome....

"What the devil's the meaning of it?" said Ivan Dmitritch, beginning to be ill-humored. "Wherever one steps, there are bits of paper under one's feet, crumbs, husks. The rooms are never swept! One is simply forced to go out. Damnation take my soul entirely! I shall go and hang myself on the first aspen tree!"

Reader Response

Chekhov's two characters show a complete range of emotion over the anticipation of winning the lottery. From laughter and happiness, they move to bitterness, hatred, and anger. Imagine that you have won a million dollars in the lottery. It will pay you $50,000 a year for twenty years. Think about your own reactions. In your response journal, respond to these questions:

a. What is your immediate reaction to the shock of suddenly becoming rich for the rest of your life? Do you celebrate in some way?

b. What will you do with the money? Are there things you have always wanted that you now set out to buy? Are there people you want to do something for immediately?

c. How does your new fortune affect your long-range plans? How will you spend the rest of your life?

d. Could your life be ruined by such wealth? Will others turn against you because of greed and envy? How will you guard against these possibilities?

COMPUTER HINT

If you are connected to an electronic mail system, forward your journal entry to a peer. Ask him or her to respond to your reactions, to raise questions you may have overlooked, to ask for clarification or explanation, to seek defense for your response.

Active Reading

"The Lottery Ticket" illustrates masterful composition. Reread the story. Notice the variety of sentence lengths Chekhov uses—some very short, some very long, some including repeated words or phrases. As you reread, use a check mark to note particularly short sentences, a star to mark long ones, and a plus to note repetition.

Studying Model Writing Techniques

Sentence Variety by Length

REMEMBER! All sorts of choices are open to you in the kinds of words and sentences you use to express yourself.

Part I: Breaking "Rules"—Short Sentences

You have probably heard the "rule": Do not write short sentences. Here is an example:

I see Spot. Spot is a dog. I see Spot run.

You can see that these are very immature sentences, the kind a young child would write. A mature writer would combine the three sentences into one:

I see the dog, Spot, running.

Exercise 1   Chekhov's shortest sentences are in dialogue form. Look only at the narrative passages and find Chekhov's five shortest sentences. Write them below.

1. _____

_____

2. _____

_____

3. _____

_____

4. _____

_____

5. _____

_____

Exercise 2   Combine each of the following series of short sentences into a single sentence. The first one has been done for you as an example.

1. Mrs. Perez is my neighbor. She is a lawyer. She is successful.

   Mrs. Perez, my neighbor, is a successful lawyer.

2. I bought gloves. They were brown. They were leather. I bought them to wear this winter.

   _____

   _____

3. There were items. The items were on sale. They were mainly canned goods. They disappeared from the shelves. They disappeared very quickly.

   _____

   _____

4. The bell rang. It rang at five o'clock. It was a signal. The signal was to stop work.

   _____

   _____

5. A painting was hung. It was hung on the wall. The wall was in the living room. The painting was by Monet.

   _____

   _____

6. Socrates was a Greek. He was a philosopher. He was great. He taught Plato.

_____

7. The *Constitution* was a ship. It was a warship. It was nicknamed "Old Ironsides." It played a role in our early history. The role was important.

_____

_____

8. Jack opened the drawer. The drawer was in the kitchen. He took out a knife. The knife was for carving. He wanted to carve the turkey.

_____

_____

9. The singer was young. The singer had long hair. He stepped into the spotlight. He tuned his guitar.

_____

_____

10. We made our way. The way was along the edge. The edge was of the river. The edge was slippery.

_____

_____

The sentences you have just rewritten are poor sentences because they are short and immature. However, not all short sentences are poor. There are times when you can and should break the "rule" and write short sentences. Such short sentences will have strength, emphasis, and interest, as the following exercise will illustrate.

Exercise 3   Revise each of the following sentences so that you have two sentences. Make one of the sentences a short sentence that adds strength, emphasis, and interest. The first two are done for you as examples.

1. All the great hustle and bustle of the day came to a complete halt and the city slept.

   All the great hustle and bustle of the day came to a complete halt. The city slept.

2. Rules are dangerous because they can close the mind to the many exceptions and lead to fatal error.

   Rules are dangerous. They can close the mind to the many exceptions and lead to fatal error.

3. He took careful aim and fired, as a result of which the cobra lay motionless.

   _____

   _____

4. Viewing movies on a VCR lets us enjoy the comforts of home while movie-going and it is a great convenience.

   _____

5. It was late at night, dark and silent, and I was half-asleep when the telephone rang.

_____

_____

6. All his years of work and planning, all his careful investments had come to nought, and he was penniless.

_____

_____

7. It was two out in the ninth inning with the bases loaded, and Willie Mays was up.

_____

_____

8. My friends had deserted me and I seemed left alone to face insurmountable problems, so I wept.

_____

_____

9. The Babe took a mighty swing at a fast ball and missed, and the Series was over.

_____

_____

10. Jeff was terribly embarrassed, blushing and stammering, while Millie just smiled.

_____

_____

Part II: Breaking "Rules"—Long Sentences

You have probably heard the "rule": Do not write very long sentences. Here is an example:

> Jogging has become very popular and it is enjoyed by young and old, and it is felt that jogging is a healthful form of exercise, but, personally, I have no desire to jog so I get my exercise by playing tennis and then I go for a swim.

You can see that this sentence is long and poorly planned. It is called a stringy sentence because ideas are carelessly strung together with words like _and, but, so,_ and _then,_ without regard to their relationship to one another. Some of these statements should be written as separate sentences, some as subordinate parts of sentences. Here is one improvement:

> Jogging has become very popular with young and old because it is thought that jogging is a healthful form of exercise. I have no desire to jog. I get my exercise by playing tennis and following up with a swim.

Exercise 4 Apparently breaking the "rules," Chekhov writes some rather long sentences.

Analyze one of them to understand why his long sentences work. One is done for you as an example:

> Example Sentence: Hatred and hope both disappeared at once, and it began immediately to seem to Ivan Dmitritch and his wife that their rooms were dark and small and low-pitched, that the supper they had been eating was not doing them good, but lying heavy on their stomachs, that the evenings were long and wearisome.
>
> Example Analysis: The sentence contains two closely related ideas: that hatred and hope disappeared and that man and wife returned to reality. The "reality" is described in a series of three word groups, each beginning with "that."

Sentence: All those wretched brothers and sisters and aunts and uncles would come crawling about as soon as they heard of the winning ticket, would begin whining like beggars, and fawning upon them with oily, hypocritical smiles.

Analysis: _____

_____

_____

_____

Exercise 5   Revise and improve each of the following stringy sentences by breaking sentences up and by subordinating some ideas.

1. Everything is peaceful at the family dinner until the talk turns to politics, and then the arguments start and everybody begins talking at once and nobody listens to anyone else so there is just a lot of useless noise.

_____

_____

_____

2. Greece was the home of the greatest of ancient civilizations, and the Greeks gave us the literature of Homer and the philosophy of Aristotle, Socrates, and Plato, and the Greeks gave us the wonderful stories of mythology and they gave us the foundations of modern science, but we must not forget the Parthenon and we must not forget the many great sculptures.

_____

_____

_____

_____

_____

3. Hard gusts of wind came and the clouds blew quickly across the darkening sky so we began to run for shelter, but the rain began to pour down and the lightning flashed so we were drenched, and we were chilled and frightened.

_____

_____

_____

_____

4. I like to watch television and my favorite programs are the news documentaries, but my kid brother always wants to watch cartoons so there is a constant war of channels and the only solution is to get another set.

_____

_____

_____

_____

5. A medicine chest should be freshly stocked and it should be neatly kept, but all medicines should be labeled correctly and any poisons should be clearly marked, but it is especially important that medicines be kept out of the reach of small children so that needless tragedy can be avoided.

_____

_____

_____

_____

_____

The sentences you have just rewritten are poor sentences because they are long and poorly planned. However, not all long sentences are poor. You can and should break the "rule" and sometimes write long, even very long, sentences. Such long sentences will be rich, flowing, and interesting. Here is an example:

> The visitor to the zoo can enjoy the antics of the monkeys, swinging wildly by their tails, making sad and comic humanlike faces, teasing the onlookers, teasing one another, chattering madly, suddenly sitting motionless and forlorn in a corner of the cage.

What is the structure of this long sentence? There is a simple statement: "The visitor to the zoo can enjoy the antics of the monkeys." This statement is followed by a long series of modifiers (participles and participial phrases) describing the antics of the monkeys.

The trick in writing a good long sentence is using a long series. Any sentence part can be expanded to a long series: the subject, the verb, the object, or any modifier (adjective, adverb, participle, prepositional phrase, infinitive phrase, or clause).

Exercise 6 Now try the following exercise in writing long sentences. First, you are given the sentence part that is to be expanded in a long series. Then you are given an example. Then you are given the beginning of another example, with the main part of the sentence and the first two items in the series. You complete the sentence by adding at least four items to the series. Be sure to include commas after each word or phrase in the series except the last.

Subject Series

Plagues, incessant wars, violent crimes, famines, treachery, plots and counterplots, oppressions, unreasonable taxation, floods, droughts, filth, and poverty marked life in Europe in the fourteenth century.

1. Purple plums, luscious pears, _____

_____

are among the rich crops of fruits and vegetables grown in California.

Verb Series

The settlers built their houses, crafted their furniture, wove their clothing, grew their food, manufactured their utensils, and buried their dead.

2. Through the years, the family loved one another, argued with no one, _____

_____

Object Series

I love the countryside, the open skies, the stretches of green meadows, the stones and rocks, the singing birds, the lakes, the rise of hills, the tall branching trees.

3. He hated the city, the noise, the crowds, _____

_____.

Adjective Series

My piano teacher was a tyrant, peremptory, stern, humorless, cold, rigid, gruff, morose, and impatient with mistakes.

4. The doctor, despite his distinguished reputation, was warm, human, _____

_____.

Participial Phrase Series

She labored all day long, reading reports, writing letters, making decisions and recommendations, supervising her department, and organizing countless details.

5. She sat in the dentist's chair, hands gripping the armrests, eyes seeing nothing, _____

_____.

Prepositional Phrase Series

They returned from their vacation and found their apartment burglarized; with drawers pulled out; with closets ransacked; with even hampers and bins emptied;

140

with clothing, papers, pencils, pots and pans, broken dishes, broken records, food, and drink strewn everywhere.

6. The empty lot was littered with rusted beer cans, with broken bottles, _____

_____

_____ .

Infinitive Series

To fly to the moon, to plumb the depths of the sea, to unlock the secret of the atom, to prevent and cure dread diseases—these have been some of the realized dreams of scientists.

7. Summer was almost here and soon she would be able to sleep late, to spend lazy afternoons on the beach, _____

_____

_____ .

Clause Series

What will the future be like if all diseases are wiped out and everybody lives hundreds of years; if we can travel at the speed of light to the distant stars; if the workweek is reduced to a few hours; if there are no jails, no hospitals, no armies?

8. Most of us can quickly forget the ice, slush, biting winds, and bitter nights when spring comes, when the robin appears, _____

_____

_____ .

Now try writing two completely original long sentences, using a series of sentence parts of your own choice.

9. _____

_____

_____

_____

_____ .

10. _____

_____

_____

_____

_____ .

Part III: Breaking the "Rules"—Repetition

You have learned earlier in this book that unnecessary repetition should be avoided. Here are some examples:

POOR: *In my opinion, I believe that swimming is the best form of exercise.*
GOOD: *In my opinion, swimming is the best form of exercise.*
GOOD: *I believe that swimming is the best form of exercise.*

POOR: *There has been a theory that the Vikings were here long before Columbus. Many people believe this theory. I believe this theory. This is a popular theory.*
GOOD: *Like many other people, I believe the popular theory that the Vikings were here long before Columbus.*

POOR: *Many people live compulsively. They live by the clock. They have a fixed time for everything. They follow a strict routine that they never depart from.*
GOOD: *Many people live by the clock.*
GOOD: *Many people rigidly follow a fixed routine.*

However, deliberate repetition of words or phrases can result in emphasis of idea and emphasis of emotion. As an example, study the sentence sequences below.

> The town I live in is dull and unattractive. It is a town of dingy brick buildings. It is a town whose skies are gray with factory smoke. It is a town of ill-stocked shops. It is a town of failing businesses. It is a town whose people lead mechanical lives. It is a town that is dying.

The writer of this passage has deliberately and skillfully repeated the words *It is a town* to emphasize the idea and emotion of the passage.

Look at another example:

> Abe Lincoln was a President who spoke words that lifted the spirits of the American people. He spoke words of brotherhood. He spoke words of faith in the future. He spoke words of hope for the common person. He spoke words of unity for the country. He spoke words of a great America.

Here again, the writer had deliberately and skillfully repeated the words *He spoke words* to emphasize the idea and emotion of the passage.

Notice that Chekhov uses some repetition, too. Consider these three examples:

> *If they were* given anything, they would ask for more; while *if they were* refused, they would swear at them, slander them, and wish them every kind of misfortune.

> She had *her own* daydreams, *her own* plans, *her own* reflections. . . .

> Ivan Dmitritch remembered his own relations, and their faces . . . struck him now as *repulsive and hateful.* . . . And his wife's face, too, struck him as *repulsive and hateful.*

Just as in a song or a chant, deliberate repetition can result in emphasis of idea and emotion. In your writing, you should occasionally deliberately repeat words in a series of sentences.

Exercise 7

1. Below are seven expressions. Choose one and write a sequence of several sentences in which the expression is deliberately repeated.

in these times	if I had my way
at the edge of the sea	when you fall in love
I will never	in the name of common sense
when I grow old	

_____

_____

_____

_____

_____

_____

_____

_____

2. Now be completely original. Choose an expression of your own to repeat in a sequence of several original sentences.

_____

_____

_____

_____

_____

_____

_____

_____

RESPONSE

Modeling

Return to your journal and read your entry about winning the lottery. Study sentence length. Remember, the response journal is informal; but as you prepare to write a formal paper, making revisions to the journal will help you create your first draft. So, make revisions in your journal entry to avoid too-short sentences except, like Chekhov, for emphasis. Check for long, stringy sentences. Can you join them more effectively? Or break them into more logical parts? Look for those wonderful long sentences with closely connected ideas like those Chekhov uses. If you find any, mark them with a star—especially if they include repetition to generate emphasis!

> ### Computer Hint
> Certain style checkers will measure sentence length, both itemized and average, for a given body of text. Using that device will let you quickly determine your own use of long and short sentences. For comparison, enter a Chekhov narrative passage for the same measure. Be aware, of course, that style checkers lack the human evaluative qualities that recognize the differences between long, stringy sentences and long, beautifully structured sentences.

Writing

With ideas from your response journal at hand, begin your first draft of an imaginative personal essay about winning a lottery. Use your imagination, have some fun, and do some serious thinking. Imagine that you have won the million-dollar lottery. It will pay you $50,000 a year for twenty years.

Although you may choose and develop your own subject, consider the following suggestions for writing your paper.

You may organize your composition as follows:

PARAGRAPH 1: *Describe in detail the events and circumstances of the winning and your immediate reactions.*

PARAGRAPH 2: *Give your short-range actions and decisions.*

PARAGRAPH 3: *Give your long-range actions and decisions.*

PARAGRAPH 4: *Conclude with parts of your response journal entry for the Reader Response questions (page 134) or with other summary thoughts you may have.*

Finally, you may want to try an experiment in style in writing this composition. If you write in the first person, referring to yourself as *I*, your composition might sound something like this:

> My family and I were people of modest means, and I, myself, had no great desire for or expectations of wealth. Out of the blue, I found myself sitting with a dozen other people, all in equal shock at being among the expectant winners of the million-dollar lottery.

Instead of writing in the first person (*I*), however, you may choose to write in the third person, referring to yourself by name and as *he* or *she*. If you wish to try this experiment, the preceding paragraph would sound like this:

> Maria and her family were people of modest means, and Maria, herself, had no great desire for or expectations of wealth. Out of the blue, Maria found herself sitting with a dozen other people, all in equal shock at being among the expectant winners of the million-dollar lottery.

As you develop this first draft, concentrate on subject matter. You will revise and proofread later.

REVISION

Now that you have finished the first draft of your imaginative personal essay about winning a lottery, you are ready to revise. In the revision process, we will focus on organization, chains of meaning, and proofreading details. Use the material as a model for your own revision process.

Checking Organization

A Whole and Its Parts

REMEMBER! Organized thinking is essential in composition writing.

An important skill of organization is to recognize and provide specific **parts** or details that make up a larger **whole**. For instance, if the whole is "a person's face," some of the parts or details are *nose, eyes, mouth,* and *chin*. If the whole is "a kitchen," some of the parts or details are *stove, sink, refrigerator,* and *cabinets*.

Chekhov names the whole picture: Dmitritch as wealthy. Then he describes the parts: well-fed, serene, healthy, warm, even hot. Then more parts, the activities: lying on his back basking in the sun, watching his children, dozing sweetly, not going to the office. Next Chekhov puts a wealthy Dmitritch through the seasons, then abroad, in each case beginning with the whole and then focusing on its parts.

The following exercises will give you practice in recognizing and providing the specific parts or details of a whole.

Exercise 8   In each of the following, you are given a whole and two of its parts. In the spaces provided, supply two additional parts.

1. library
   card catalog   stacks   _____   _____

2. tree
   bark   roots   _____   _____

3. sailboat
   rigging   rudder   _____   _____

4. corn
   husk   silk   _____   _____

5. army
   officers   tanks   _____   _____

Exercise 9   In each of the following, you are given a whole and one part. In the spaces provided, supply three additional parts.

1. letter
   inside address   _____   _____   _____

2. bicycle
   handlebars   _____   _____   _____

3. fishing tackle
   lure

   _____   _____   _____

4. discotheque
   dance floor

   _____   _____   _____

5. bird
   wings

   _____   _____   _____

Exercise 10   In each of the following, you are given only a whole. In the spaces provided, supply four parts.

1. newspaper

_____   _____   _____   _____

2. bed

_____   _____   _____   _____

3. beach

_____   _____   _____   _____

4. zoo

_____   _____   _____   _____

5. leg

_____   _____   _____   _____

Modeling

Turn to your draft of your personal essay about winning the lottery. Make a list of the whole ideas included in your draft. Then make a list, similar to those in the exercises above, that detail the parts. Ask a peer editor to help. If the two of you have trouble completing the list, you probably need to revise to include the parts.

COMPUTER HINT

Use the keyboard to generate your "list." Although it may be a bit unconventional to do so, you may wish to use the bold command to highlight key words (the "whole") and the underscore to denote the parts. You will then be able to tell immediately where "parts" are missing.

Checking Chains of Meaning

Details—A Whole and Its Parts

REMEMBER! In composition writing, sentences are not individual or isolated. Instead, the thought is carried along from sentence to sentence in a chain of meaning.

In the previous unit, you learned that a generalization supported by specific examples is an important thought form that can shape the chain of meaning of a sentence sequence. Another such important thought form is a generalization (a whole) supported by concrete **details** (the parts of a whole).

Chekhov uses the entire story "The Lottery Ticket" to give parts of the whole: "To torment and tantalize oneself with hopes of possible fortune is so sweet, so thrilling." The remainder of the story details the parts of the torment.

Look at the following general statements.

_____ **1.** The kitchen, often one of the smaller rooms of a house, is usually the most richly supplied and equipped.

_____ **2.** Lying in bed, even on a quiet night, one can hear a variety of sounds.

_____ **3.** A book has a number of important parts that we sometimes overlook.

_____ **4.** A coral reef is an association of many forms of life.

_____ **5.** It was a dismal February day.

The following are statements of parts—concrete details:

a. The table of contents summarizes the subject matter and outlines the organization. The index helps you to locate specific topics in which you are interested. In some cases, the copyright date is important.

b. It is there that such appliances as the stove, refrigerator, sink, and dishwasher are found. The cabinets and closets are stocked with food, dishes, utensils, and dishwasher detergents.

c. The sky was a low-lying blanket of dull gray. The bare trees shivered in the cold gusts that blew from the north. A damp chill penetrated the bones of the few people in the streets.

d. There are the many species of the coral itself. Worms, mollusks, algae, starfish, sponges, and sea urchins are also part of the complex.

e. The ticking of the clock is loud in the night. A passing plane roars by. The distant voices of persons in the street are heard. Somewhere a door slams shut.

Generalizations by themselves can be vague and unconvincing. Details by themselves can lack broader meaning. But when you put the generalization and the specific details together, you have a strong, useful thought form that can shape the chain of meaning of a sentence sequence.

Exercise 11   Each of the five generalizations (1–5) goes with one of the five statements of specific details (*a–e*). Match them to provide a sentence sequence. In the space provided alongside each generalization, write the letter of the matching statements of details.

Exercise 12   Now try your hand at writing your own generalization to form a chain of meaning with given statements of details. In the space provided, write a good general statement to form a sentence sequence with the following given statements of details.

1. _____

   His coat was like long strands of golden silk. His large, gentle brown eyes were set in a perfectly formed, proud head. His tail wagged gently as he extended a friendly paw.

2. _____

   The battery, oil level, and tire pressure should be checked regularly. Windshield wipers should be changed periodically. Tires, belts, and hoses should be replaced before they break and cause trouble.

3. _____

   Her great sails, seeming to tower to the sky, bellowed in the wind. Her bow threw up great sprays. A churning wake streamed behind her.

4. _____

   Smaller groups and individuals pushed this way and that, wildly aimless. They shouted and cursed and screamed. They waved their placards and signs. Their faces were twisted with hate and anger.

5. _____

   The leather was glove-soft. The toe was rounded and roomy and the heel sensibly flat. The neutral gray was a practical color, given life by the small green insets. The simple design was flattering to the foot.

6. _____

   The clean salt breeze coming off the water stimulates and refreshes. The soft sand is a comfort to tired feet. The rhythmic ebb and flow of the waves and the soaring, wheeling gulls soothe the eye and ear.

7. _____

My feet ached. My head hurt. My muscles felt as though I had been kicked by a mule. I was covered with grime and sweat.

8. _____

_____

The large pink petals were softly curved. At the center was a great golden eye. The fragrance was delicately sweet.

9. _____

_____

Broken glass spattered the road along with great chunks of twisted metal. Oil and blood puddled the concrete. We heard, in the distance, the siren of an ambulance.

10. _____

_____

_____

The surface was a smooth mirror, broken here and there near the shores with patches of water lilies. A lone duck seemed to be asleep on the glass. The only sound was the hum of crickets.

Exercise 13 Now try the reverse. Each sentence given below is a general statement. Form a sentence sequence by adding statements of appropriate specific details. You can add one, two, or three sentences to form each sentence sequence.

1. In the center of the lawn stood a magnificent tree.

_____

_____

_____

_____

2. The singer stepped into the spotlight.

_____

_____

_____

_____

3. The street was filthy.

_____

_____

_____

_____

4. The motorcycle was a startling sight.

_____

_____

_____

5. It was a typical Sunday at the pool.

_____

_____

_____

6. The meal was superb.

_____

_____

7. A woman of strange appearance stood on the corner.

_____

_____

_____

8. The fruits and vegetables in the market looked good.

_____

_____

_____

9. My friend looked awful.

_____

_____

_____

10. The room I stepped into obviously belonged to a tidy person.

_____

_____

_____

Modeling

Turn now to your work in progress. Look for the parts—the details that make up the larger whole. For example, notice how Chekhov gives first the whole, that Ivan Dmitritch dreams, with pictures "crowding his imagination, each more gracious and poetical than the last." Then he follows with the parts—all of the details of Ivan's dreams: how he feels, what he does, how he looks, where he lives, where he bathes, what he eats and drinks. Follow Chekhov's model to revise your own personal essay. A peer editor may be able to offer objective advice about areas of revision.

Proofreading

As you proofread for errors in spelling and punctuation, you should also take note of the two common errors emphasized here for your attention: misplaced modifiers and dangling participles. The exercises that follow will help you to recognize and avoid these errors in your writing.

Misplaced Modifiers

Look at the following group of three sentences. All three sentences have exactly the same words. All three are correct. What is the difference among them?

The man, riding a bicycle, accidentally knocked over an old woman.
Riding a bicycle, the man accidentally knocked over an old woman.
The man accidentally knocked over an old woman riding a bicycle.

The difference among these three sentences is that the modifying phrase "riding a bicycle" occurs in a different position in each sentence. In the first and second sentences, the meaning is the same because the modifying phrase occurs closest to the word it modifies—*man*. The third sentence, however, has a different meaning entirely because the phrase occurs closest to the word *woman* and is therefore understood to modify *woman*.

You can place modifying words and phrases at different positions in a sentence, but you must make sure that you place modifiers so that they make the sense you want. If you will look now at three different sentences, you will see that there can be plenty of trouble with the placement of the modifiers.

In a store window, we saw a stool for a pianist with three legs.
Treasure Island is a story about a pirate with one leg named Long John Silver.
I saw them leave before the sun came up in a red car.

The writers of these sentences have placed modifying phrases in such a way as to create some unintentional strange meanings. In the first sentence, the pianist has three legs. In the second sentence, one of the pirate's legs is named Long John Silver. In the third sentence, the sun comes up in a red car. These sentences can easily be improved by moving the modifiers to a more sensible position and making other minor adjustments.

In a store window, we saw a pianist's stool with three legs.
Treasure Island is a story about a pirate named Long John Silver, who had one leg.
Before the sun came up, I saw them leave in a red car.

Exercise 14   Revise each of the following sentences to correct the unintended ridiculous meaning.

1. The Lincoln Memorial was built to honor a great president who was assassinated as a token of the nation's esteem.

_____

_____

2. Be sure to buy enough wool to finish your sweater before you start knitting.

_____

_____

3. Manufacturers are trying to develop injury-proof helmets for football players made of plastic.

_____

_____

4. Lucy watched the favorite win the Kentucky Derby wearing a cashmere sweater.

_____

_____

5. The newspaper lists the names of couples who have been recently engaged for a small fee.

_____

_____

6. The corrupt politician was indicted for a long list of crimes by the district attorney.

_____

_____

7. The caravan traveled across desert wasteland on camels extending over 500 miles.

_____

_____

8. We paid the doctor for the operation he had performed by mail.

_____

_____

9. He bought a watch for his sister-in-law, a cheap-looking thing.

_____

_____

10. The fire was put out before any damage was done by the local fire department.

_____

_____

_____

Dangling Participles

One form of modifier is the participle or participial phrase. Frequently, a sentence will begin with such a modifier. The participle or participial phrase is then understood to modify the first noun or pronoun that follows it. In the following sentences, the participial modifier is italicized and the modified word is underlined.

Having finished the meal, the <u>family</u> relaxed and chatted.
Fired from his job, <u>Mr. Smith</u> was in despair.
Rising with a powerful thrust, the <u>rocket</u> soared upward.

However, if you look at the next three sentences, you will see that something is wrong. In each of these sentences, if the participial modifier is understood to modify the first noun or pronoun that follows, the meaning is ridiculous. The participial modifier is **dangling.**

Growing green and lush, the neighbors admired the lawn.
Having done the wash, the dinner was prepared by my brother.
Walking beside the lake, a fish suddenly jumped out of the water.

These sentences can be made more sensible by revising them so that a suitable noun or pronoun follows the participial modifier.

Growing green and lush, the lawn was admired by the neighbors.
Having done the wash, my brother prepared the dinner.
Walking beside the lake, I saw a fish jump suddenly out of the water.

Exercise 15   Revise each of the following sentences to eliminate the dangling participial modifier. The first two are done for you as examples.

1. Being a freshman, Shakespeare meant little to him.

   Being a freshman, he saw little meaning in Shakespeare.

2. Sweating profusely, the disabled truck was pushed off the highway by the driver.

   Sweating profusely, the driver pushed the disabled truck off the highway.

3. Having finished our meal, the waiter gave us the check.

   _____

   _____

4. Reading the newspaper, the dog was heard to bark suddenly by Pedro.

   _____

   _____

5. Listening to the compact disc player, the orchestra seemed to be in the room with us.

   _____

   _____

6. Sitting in the grandstand, the horses were cheered on by the crowd.

   _____

   _____

7. Having moved at fifteen, his hometown was no longer familiar to him.

_____

_____

8. Cleaning the garage, my head was badly bumped on the shelf.

_____

_____

9. Climbing the mountain, the town came into view.

_____

_____

10. Losing her temper, the mirror was smashed by Wilma.

_____

_____

Modeling

After you have gone through the exercises, return to the literary model. Notice Chekhov's use of modifiers, including participles. Can you readily identify the antecedent for each? Notice where each appears in relationship to its antecedent. Consider these model sentences from the story:

a. *Unable to believe his eyes*, he hurriedly dropped the paper on his knees. . . .

b. *Looking at his wife*, Ivan Dmitritch gave a broad, senseless smile. . . .

c. Ivan Dmitritch, *holding the paper in his hand*, walked several times from corner to corner. . . .

d. "Yes, an estate, that would be nice," said his wife, *sitting down and dropping her hands in her lap*.

e. His little boy and girl are crawling about near him, *digging in the sand or catching ladybirds in the grass*.

f. Or, *tired of lying still*, he goes to the hayfield. . . .

When you have finished the exercises and studied the model, give your composition a final proofreading.

Peer or Self-Evaluation Guide

Before you prepare a final copy of your imaginative personal essay about winning a lottery, ask a peer or peers to read it and use the following guidelines for offering suggestions. Or use the guidelines as a means of self-evaluation.

	very well	1	2	3	4	poorly
1. How well does the essay create emphasis with sentence length—using long sentences, short sentences, sentences with repetition?						
2. How well does the writer organize the essay, arranging the parts as details of the whole?						
3. How well does the writer use chains of meaning, moving from the whole to its parts?						
4. How well does the writer avoid misplaced modifiers?						
5. How well does the writer avoid dangling participles?						

The Final Draft: Sharing

Before you prepare your final draft for the publishing stage, take into consideration your peers' suggestions and/or your self-evaluation based on the guidelines above. Add a title. Then read again to check for final details.

Unit 9

A Research Article About Gold

PREWRITING

Reading the Literature

Gold has fascinated the world for centuries. Nations have based their monetary systems on it. Talented artists stake their names to it. The finest gems are mounted in it. The informative literary selection which follows, however, may include details about gold you've never heard. So, as you read to enjoy the fascinating details about this precious element, try to identify some aspect of gold about which you'd like to know more. Perhaps some idea in J. Bronowski's article will pique your curiosity.

GOLD by J. Bronowski

For reasons which are oblique but not accidental, alchemy was much occupied with another metal, gold, which is virtually useless. Yet gold has so fascinated human societies that I should be perverse if I did not try to isolate the properties that gave it its symbolic power.

Gold is the universal prize in all countries, in all cultures, in all ages. A representative collection of gold artifacts reads like a chronicle of civilizations. Enameled gold rosary, sixteenth century, English. Gold serpent brooch, 400 B.C., Greek. Triple gold crown of Abuna, seventeenth century, Abyssinian. Gold snake bracelet, ancient Roman. Ritual vessels of Achaemenid gold, sixth century B.C., Persian. Drinking bowl of Malik gold, eighth century B.C., Persian. Bulls' heads in gold ... Ceremonial gold knife, Chimu, Pre-Inca, Peruvian, ninth century ...

Sculpted gold saltcellar, Benvenuto Cellini, sixteenth-century figures, made for King Francis I. Cellini recalled what his French patron said of it:

When I set this work before the king, he gasped in amazement and could not take his eyes off it. He cried in astonishment, "This is a hundred times more heavenly than I would ever have thought! What a marvel the man is!"

The Spaniards plundered Peru for its gold, which the Inca aristocracy had collected as we might collect stamps, with the touch of Midas. Gold for greed, gold for splendor, gold for adornment, gold for reverence, gold for power, sacrificial gold, life-giving gold, gold for tenderness, barbaric gold, voluptuous gold . . .

The Chinese put their finger on what made it irresistible. Ko-Hung said, "Yellow gold, if melted a hundred times, will not be spoiled." In that phrase we become aware that gold has a physical quality that makes it singular; which can be tested or assayed in practice, and characterized in theory.

It is easy to see that the man who made a gold artifact was not just a technician, but an artist. But it is equally important, and not so easy to recognize, that the man who assayed gold was also more than a technician. To him gold was an element of science. Having a technique is useful but, like every skill, what brings it to life is its place in a general scheme of nature—a theory.

Men who tested and refined gold made visible a theory of nature: a theory in which gold was unique, and yet might be made from other elements. That is why so much of antiquity spent its time and ingenuity in devising tests for pure gold. Francis Bacon at the opening of the seventeenth century put the issue squarely.

> Gold hath these natures: greatness of weight, closeness of parts, fixation, pliantness or softness, immunity from rust, color or tincture of yellow. If a man can make a metal that hath all these properties, let men dispute whether it be gold or no.

Among the several classical tests for gold, one in particular makes the diagnostic property most visible. This is a precise test by cupellation. A bone-ash vessel, or cupel, is heated in the furnace and brought up to a temperature much higher than pure gold requires. The gold, with its impurities or dross, is put in the vessel and melts. (Gold has quite a low melting point, just over 1000°C, almost the same as copper.) What happens now is that the dross leaves the gold and is absorbed into the walls of the vessel: so that all at once there is a visible separation between, as it were, the dross of this world and the hidden purity of the gold in the flame. The dream of the alchemists, to make synthetic gold, has in the end to be tested by the reality of the pearl of gold that survives the assay.

The ability of gold to resist what was called decay (what we would call chemical attack) was singular, and therefore both valuable and diagnostic. It also carried a powerful symbolism, which is explicit even in the earliest formulae. The first written reference we have to alchemy is just over two thousand years old, and comes from China. It tells how to make gold and to use it to prolong life. That is an extraordinary conjunction to us. To us gold is precious because it is scarce; but to the alchemists, all over the world, gold was precious because it was incorruptible. No acid or alkali known to those times would attack it. That indeed is how the emperor's goldsmiths assayed or, as they would have said, parted it, by an acid treatment that was less laborious than cupellation.

When life was thought to be (and for most people was) solitary, poor, nasty, brutish, and short, to the alchemists gold represented the one eternal spark in the human body. Their search to make gold and to find the elixir of life are one and the same endeavor. Gold is the symbol of immortality—but I ought not to say symbol, because in the thought of the alchemists gold was the expression, the embodiment of incorruptibility, in the physical and in the living world together.

So when the alchemists tried to transmute base metals into gold, the transformation that they sought in the fire was from the corruptible to the incorruptible; they were trying to extract the quality of permanence from the everyday. And this was the same as the search for eternal youth: every medicine to fight old age contained gold, metallic gold, as an essential ingredient, and the alchemists urged their patrons to drink from gold cups to prolong life.

from *The Ascent of Man*

Reader Response

Consider the many details about gold that Bronowski presents in the excerpt from *The Ascent of Man*: historical artifacts, synthetic gold, plundering and war, alchemy tests, eternal youth. These details, fanciful enough to stir the reader's imagination, should trigger questions. In your response journal, write as many questions as you can about gold. Perhaps your questions spring directly from something Bronowski says, perhaps from personal experience, perhaps from just a matter of curiosity. Your questions may range from the serious to the fanciful, from the practical to the impractical, from the personal to the generic. Try for at least ten questions.

When you have completed your list of questions (or depleted your imagination), share your list with at least two peers. Use the activity as the beginning of a brainstorming session. What additional questions do your peers' questions raise for you? Add them to the list.

Finally, share your combined lists with those from the rest of the class. Typically, the combined questions will suggest a wide array of issues about gold.

> ### COMPUTER HINT
> As you and your classmates combine lists, generate a composite at the keyboard and provide copies for all. Or, if you are networked, simply send your lists to one another or to a master terminal from which a composite can be printed.

Active Reading

A writer creates an identifiable style by the kinds of words and sentences he or she chooses to use. For instance, Bronowski begins with "For reasons which are *oblique* but not accidental, alchemy was much occupied with another metal, gold. . . . I should be *perverse* if I did not try to *isolate the properties* that gave it its *symbolic power*." He could just as well have said, "For reasons which are *roundabout* but not accidental, alchemy was much occupied with another metal, gold. . . . I should be *in error* if I did not try to *separate the aspects* that gave it its *representative strength."* He did not, however, choose those synonyms. Thus, he created his personal style.

Skim the Bronowski selection again. This time pay particular attention to his word choices. Lightly underscore words which seem to separate Bronowski from other authors whose works you've read in this text.

Studying Model Writing Techniques

Diction

REMEMBER! All sorts of choices are open to you in the kinds of words and sentences you use to express yourself.

Whenever you write or speak, you choose words to express your meanings. **Diction** refers to the choice of words that you make. In any situation, there are usually several different ways of expressing a meaning. For example, look at the following pair of sentences.

I fell and hurt my kneecap.
The orthopedist said that I had injured my patella.

The words *kneecap* and *patella* mean the same thing. *Kneecap* is an everyday, familiar word while *patella* is technical and formal. There are many occasions when you will have a choice between such words in your writing. There are times when the familiar word will be appropriate and times when the formal or technical word will be appropriate.

COMPUTER HINT

If you have computer access to a thesaurus, you will find valuable assistance there in selecting the precise diction for your own work. Be aware, however, that synonyms carry different shades of meaning. Always check the dictionary definition for a synonym before you use it, perhaps incorrectly.

Exercise 1 Here is a list of formal or technical words from Bronowski's selection "Gold." Give a familiar, everyday equivalent for each word.

1. chronicle _____

2. splendor _____

3. adornment _____

4. reverence _____

5. sacrificial _____

6. barbaric _____

7. voluptuous _____

8. singular _____

9. assayed _____

10. ingenuity _____

11. diagnostic _____

12. dross _____

13. explicit _____

14. conjunction _____

15. incorruptible _____

16. brutish _____

17. elixir _____

18. endeavor _____

19. embodiment _____

20. transmute _____

Exercise 2   Choose any three pairs of words from Exercise 1. Write an original sentence in which each word of the pair is used suitably.

1. _____

_____

2. _____

_____

3. _____

_____

4. _____

_____

5. _____

_____

6. _____

_____

Exercise 3   Try this exercise in exact vocabulary. You are given five headings for specialized vocabularies. How many words can you list that are appropriate to each heading? You are given two words to get you started on each list.

1. How many birds can you name?

   condor _____   _____   _____

thrush _____ _____ _____

_____ _____ _____

_____ _____ _____

2. How many different kinds of ships or boats can you name?

galleon _____ _____ _____

rowboat _____ _____ _____

_____ _____ _____

_____ _____ _____

3. How many tools can you name?

jackhammer _____ _____ _____

rasp _____ _____ _____

4. How many exact colors can you name?

scarlet _____ _____ _____

turquoise _____ _____ _____

_____ _____ _____

_____ _____ _____

5. How many kinds of dogs can you name?

Pekinese _____ _____ _____

bloodhound _____ _____ _____

_____ _____ _____

_____ _____ _____

Exercise 4 In this exercise you are to supply words and phrases associated with specialized fields. Supply as many terms as you can.

1. How many legal terms can you list?

plaintiff _____ _____ _____

deed _____ _____ _____

_____ _____ _____

2. How many cooking terms can you list?

simmer _____ _____ _____

broil _____ _____ _____

_____ _____ _____

3. How many music terms can you list?

harmony _____ _____ _____

sonata _____ _____ _____

_____ _____ _____

4. How many art terms can you list?

palette _____ _____ _____

lithograph _____ _____ _____

_____ _____ _____

5. How many terms pertaining to feudalism and the Middle Ages can you list?

serf _____ _____ _____

liege _____ _____ _____

_____ _____ _____

Exercise 5 Choose any one of the lists in Exercises 3 and 4. Write an interesting, original sentence sequence (three to five sentences) in which you use several words from the list you selected.

_____

_____

_____

_____

_____

_____

_____

_____

_____

RESPONSE

Modeling

Review the list of questions you and your classmates formulated during the Reader Response activity. Study the diction choices in the composite list. Does the diction seem to be affected by the content of the question? For instance, are serious questions couched in diction different from that for fanciful questions? In other words, do you use more dignified words and phrases for serious than you do for fanciful questions? What generalizations can you make about diction and its relationship to content and style? In other words, does the writer's word choice help the reader to recognize fanciful content or humorous style?

Writing

Frequently writers address topics that interest them but about which they need additional information to write intelligently. Thus, the research article commonly appears in literature. Your assignment in this unit is to write a research article. The assignment implies that you do not know enough just yet to set about writing this composition. You will first have to collect information and facts. How will you do this? Consider these guidelines:

First, you must narrow the topic. You and your classmates have already explored a number of questions about gold, matters of curiosity for which someone, at least, wants answers. So, on the one hand, you may now select one guiding question for which you will seek an answer. The answer will be part of your research article about gold.

On the other hand, you may want to continue to explore the broad topic of gold, doing general reading in search of a specific topic that interests you. There are many possibilities.

You may wish to limit yourself to discussing a few fascinating but little-known facts about gold. Or you may want to write about practical uses of gold in modern times. You may wish to discuss gold as a symbol, as in royal crowns, wedding bands, and medals of honor. You may want to write about one event, such as the Gold Rush, or one place, such as South Africa. You may decide to write about gold coins or buried treasure or gold in biblical times. You may prefer to deal with stories about gold, such as "King Midas" and "Jack and the Beanstalk." You may wish to write about the alchemists, who tried to turn lead into gold. These are but a few of the many possible ways in which you can narrow your topic.

Next, go to the library prepared to take notes. Select a good encyclopedia, look up the article on gold, read the article, and take notes on information related to your question or narrowed topic. Remember to *avoid copying verbatim* from the article. Copying someone else's words and calling them your own is called *plagiarism* and is considered a serious academic offense. In addition, be sure to keep track of the sources from which you gather information. You will need to acknowledge them in the text of your paper.

When you finish this first article, check for a list at the end which names related subjects referring you to other articles with additional information on gold. Read those and take more notes, being certain, again, to paraphrase or summarize, not copy words or phrases directly from the source.

When you have finished the process, select a second encyclopedia and repeat the reading and note taking.

You may also wish to take a third step. With the help of the card catalog or computer catalog and the librarian, you can locate books that contain sections dealing with the topic of gold. You can browse through one or two of these books and do some additional note taking.

Having completed your job of note taking, you will need to mull over the information you have gathered on your guiding question or narrowed topic and decide on a way to treat the topic. Once that is decided, the organization of your composition will be almost automatic. In the first paragraph, you will simply want to introduce the topic and arouse the reader's interest. In the second and third paragraphs—the body of your composition—you will present the information you have gathered and selected. In your fourth and final paragraph, you will summarize or come to some conclusion.

Many things other than gold have played an important and dramatic role in the human story. Some of these are diamonds, coal, iron, oil, stone, wood, water, fire, electricity, and the horse. You may wish to choose one of these as the topic of your composition instead of gold. If you do so, proceed with the same steps of research, note taking, and limiting the topic.

> ### COMPUTER HINT
> Depending on the facilities in your research center, you may be able to consult computerized references, especially those on CD ROM. The indexing system for such references will speed your search for specific information. Do not, however, plan to use a networked computer search service. Such services should be reserved for sophisticated, technical research otherwise unavailable. For this topic adequate information is readily available.

When you are ready to write your first draft, be certain that you do not plagiarize. The words in your paper must be your own even though you will, of course, give credit to your sources. You may use a parenthetical note in the MLA style for a signed article (Luciana Chiappini, "Este, House of," *Encyclopaedia Britannica*: *Macropaedia*, 1974 ed.) or for an unsigned article ("Melodeon," *Encyclopedia Americana*, 1985 ed.). Or use whatever form your instructor prefers.

REVISION

Now that you have finished the first draft of your research article, you are ready to revise. In the revision process, we will focus on organization, chains of meaning, and proofreading details. Use the materials as a model for your own revision process.

Checking Organization

A Whole and Its Parts

REMEMBER! Organized thinking is essential in composition writing.

As in the preceding unit, you will deal with a **whole** and its **parts.** An important skill of organization is to be able to recognize and supply a whole that is suggested by a list of specific parts. For instance, if you are given the parts *knee, ankle, calf,* and *thigh,* you would recognize that the whole that encompasses all of these parts is "leg."

Bronowski gives us many "parts" of gold, the whole. He gives us history, art, emotion, tests, and alchemy. Writers often organize their compositions from whole to part or from part to whole. How do you think Bronowski organizes his selection?

Exercise 6   In the exercise that follows, you will be given four parts for each item. Supply the whole to which the parts belong.

1. mats   parallel bars
   ropes   floor   _____

164

2. bride   ushers
   rice   ring   _____

3. monitor   keyboard
   disk drive mouse   _____

4. fish   filter
   plants   gravel   _____

5. directors shareholders
   president dividends   _____

6. stage   curtain
   footlights seats   _____

7. keys   correction tape
   ribbon   roller   _____

8. speaker tape deck
   tuner   turntable   _____

9. foul lines mound
   bases   plate   _____

10. lining   sleeves
    buttons lapels   _____

11. bed   mouth
    source   banks   _____

12. beds   nurses
    doctors operating room _____

13. congress cabinet
    president courts   _____

Modeling

Check the draft of your research article. Compare your organization with that in the Bronowski article. Have you organized your paper so that your reader can recognize and supply a whole that is suggested or explained by specific parts? Do you present the parts in a logical, sequential way? If possible, ask a peer or peers to read your paper and respond to these same questions. Revise as necessary.

Checking Chains of Meaning

Details—A Whole and Its Characteristics

REMEMBER! In composition writing, sentences are not individual or isolated. Instead, the thought is carried along from sentence to sentence in a chain of meaning.

In the following sentence sequence from the Bronowski selection, a generalization is supported by details that name or describe the parts of a whole. Reread the passage:

> Gold is the universal prize in all countries, in all cultures, in all ages. A representative collection of gold artifacts reads like a chronicle of civilizations. Enam-

eled gold rosary, sixteenth century, English. Gold serpent brooch, 400 B.C., Greek. Triple gold crown of Abuna, seventeenth century, Abyssinian. . . .

Here is another passage:

> A bouquet of flowers stood in a vase on the table. The bright red of long-stemmed roses dominated the center. Around the roses were irises of sparkling blue. Hanging over the rim of the vase were sprays of lily of the valley.

Exercise 7 Refer to the preceding paragraph.

1. Write the sentence that contains the general statement.

_____

2. List three supporting details.

a. _____

_____

b. _____

_____

c. _____

_____

Here is another sentence sequence that begins with the same general statement as the preceding sequence.

> A bouquet of flowers stood in a vase on the table. Their gentle fragrance filled the room. They expressed a sense of love and beauty in the house.

You can see that this passage begins with the same general statement as the first. You can see also that the three sentences form a coherent sequence. However, the details of this sequence, unlike those of the first passage, do not describe or identify parts of the whole. If the "fragrance" and the "sense of love and beauty" are not parts of the whole, then what are they? What is the thought form of this sentence sequence?

A little thought will tell you that "fragrance" and "sense of love and beauty" are **characteristics** of the whole, as contrasted with parts of the whole.

Exercise 8 Below are five pairs of short sentence sequences. Each pair begins with the same general statement. In each pair of sequences, the thought form of one sequence is details (a whole and its parts), and the thought form of the other sequence is details (a whole and its characteristics). In the spaces provided, place a check next to the whole and its parts sequences. Place a zero next to the whole and its characteristics sequences.

_____ **1.** The housefly is a common insect. It is attracted to garbage and buzzes unpleasantly.

_____ **2.** The housefly is a common insect. It has two transparent wings, compound eyes, antennae, and three pairs of legs.

166

_____ **3.** California is one of our great states. It offers natural beauty of every kind and an attractive climate.

_____ **4.** California is one of our great states. It includes the cities of Los Angeles and San Francisco, the Sierra Nevada Mountains, and the Imperial Valley.

_____ **5.** Four dogs were in the kennel. One was a large, old black poodle; another, a tiny Chihuahua; the remaining two, mongrels.

_____ **6.** Four dogs were in the kennel. They were depressed and sickly looking.

_____ **7.** The old house stood before us. It had an air of mystery and danger.

_____ **8.** The old house stood before us. The door hung on rusty hinges, the windows were boarded up, and the chimney had collapsed.

_____ **9.** Everyone liked the officer at the crossing. She was cheerful, friendly, and considerate.

_____ **10.** Everyone liked the officer at the crossing. She had blue eyes, chestnut hair, and a dazzling smile.

Exercise 9 Now try your hand at writing your own general statement to form a chain of meaning with given statements of characteristics. In the space provided, write a good general statement to form a sentence sequence with the given statements of characteristics which follow.

1. _____

_____

It is rich yellow in color. It is a metal that is soft and easily shaped. It does not corrode. Great value has always been placed on it.

2. _____

_____

Their air smells with pollution. Their streets are filthy. Neither the ordinary person on the sidewalks nor the banks are safe from criminal attack.

3. _____

_____

He is big and strong, yet incredibly quick and graceful on his feet. He is confident and aggressive.

4. _____

_____

It is a nation that values the rights and freedom of every individual. Equal education for all is considered fundamental. The oppressed of other lands have always been welcomed.

5. _____

_____

The fibers can be woven into many kinds of fabrics, all durable, warm, and attractive. The supply is plentiful and self-renewing.

6. _____

They are beautiful in color and in movement. They devour harmful insects by the billions. They are an aid in cross-pollination. We admire their cheerful song and graceful flight.

7. _____

Her costumes and makeup are weird. Her gyrations on the stage are frenzied. The sounds she produces make her audiences go wild.

8. _____

They are independent and fixed in their ways. They can be endlessly lazy or tirelessly active, mean and nasty or playful and charming. They are deadly to mice. Their curiosity is so great that it has sometimes been said to be the death of them.

9. _____

It comes in many varieties, each with its own distinctive smell and taste, from the mild Swiss to the tangy Gorgonzola. It is highly nutritious, plentiful, and delicious.

10. _____

The melody is haunting and unforgettable. The words speak to everyone who has ever been in love.

Exercise 10 Now try the reverse. Each of the following sentences is a general statement. Form a sentence sequence by adding statements of characteristics. You can add one, two, or three sentences to form each sentence sequence. Be sure to give characteristics, not parts of the whole!

1. Everyone likes our boss.

_____

_____

2. Fruits and vegetables are an important part of the diet.

_____

_____

3. I love the autumn.

_____

_____

_____

4. Dogs make the best pets.

_____

_____

_____

5. Let me tell you about my little brother.

_____

_____

_____

6. A salesman stood at the door.

_____

_____

_____

7. The new car was delivered.

_____

_____

_____

8. We liked the movie.

_____

_____

_____

9. The crowd stared at the shark in the aquarium tank.

_____

_____

_____

_____

10. The school cafeteria was in its usual state.

_____

_____

_____

Modeling

As you know, generating adequate details in a piece of writing is often the greatest stumbling block for writers. Reread your draft. Mark the sentences which you consider generalizations. Next, ask yourself if details follow—details that either name or describe the parts or characterize the whole. Check your paper against the model literary selection and the examples in the exercises. Ask a peer editor or editors to help if you find your own paper difficult to analyze. Then revise as necessary.

Proofreading

As you proofread for errors in spelling and punctuation, you should take special note of the two common errors emphasized for your attention: parallel structure and comparison. The exercises that follow will help you to recognize and avoid these errors in your writing.

Parallel Structure

Look at these sentences.

Miranda swims. Miranda skates. Miranda jogs. Miranda dances.

You can see that each sentence has the same subject—*Miranda*—and a different verb. Since all the verbs are related to the same subject in the same way, the four sentences can be written as one.

Miranda swims, skates, jogs, and dances.

This sentence can be depicted this way:

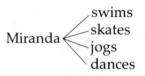

As the diagram shows, the four verbs in the sentence are parallel; they relate to the rest of the sentence in the same way. When parts of a sentence are parallel, they should be in the same grammatical form.

Note this sentence, a poor one:

Miranda swims, skates, jogs, and she is a dancer.

In this sentence, the three verbs are followed by a complete independent clause. The parallel parts of the sentence are no longer in parallel grammatical form.

Study the following illustrations:

NONPARALLEL:	*The new car was both economical and a beauty.* [adjective and noun]
PARALLEL:	*The new car was both economical and beautiful.* [two adjectives]
NONPARALLEL:	*They liked to play tennis, to surf, and sailing.* [two infinitives and a gerund]
PARALLEL:	*They liked to play tennis, to surf, and to sail.* [three infinitives]
PARALLEL:	*They liked playing tennis, surfing, and sailing.* [three gerunds]
NONPARALLEL:	*He asked us for money and if we could give him advice.* [prepositional phrase, dependent clause]
PARALLEL:	*He asked us for money and for advice.* [two prepositional phrases]

NONPARALLEL: *James told the counselor about his illness, that he was planning to leave, and other personal matters.* [prepositional phrase, dependent clause, noun]

PARALLEL: *James told the counselor about his illness, his plans for leaving, and other personal matters.* [three nouns]

Exercise 11   Of the following sentences, seven are written in nonparallel structure and three are written in parallel structure. Revise the seven faulty sentences so that the structure is parallel. Leave the others alone.

1. He called for her punctually, gave her flowers, and took her out to the taxi.

2. My uncle's ambition was to retire and living as a man of leisure.

3. Frances asked her parents for money and whether she could use the car.

4. The radio is small, compact, and can be bought inexpensively.

5. The applicants were told to write in ink and that they should print legibly.

6. You can get to the store either by train or a bus can be taken.

7. The scientist was fascinated by the possibility of traveling to other planets and finding life on them.

8. The magazine article was inaccurate, misleading, and unclear.

9. The city can disturb country people with its crowds, its confusion, and because of the noise.

_____

_____

10. The best way to teach children is not by threatening them but to explain things patiently.

_____

_____

Comparison

We frequently use comparison in our writing. There are several common errors to watch out for in comparison structures.

Review the word forms that help us express the three degrees of comparison: positive, comparative, and superlative.

Some words add *-er* and *-est* to form the comparative and superlative degrees.

Positive	Comparative	Superlative
cool	cooler	coolest
sweet	sweeter	sweetest
cheap	cheaper	cheapest
happy	happier	happiest
healthy	healthier	healthiest
lovely	lovelier	loveliest

Some words add *more* and *most*.

Positive	Comparative	Superlative
agile	more agile	most agile
convenient	more convenient	most convenient
recent	more recent	most recent
swiftly	more swiftly	most swiftly
boldly	more boldly	most boldly
frequently	more frequently	most frequently

Some words have their own special forms.

Positive	Comparative	Superlative
bad	worse	worst
good	better	best
little	less	least
many	more	most
much	more	most
well	better	best

Negative comparisons are formed by adding *less* and *least*.

Positive	Comparative	Superlative
successful	less successful	least successful
expensive	less expensive	least expensive
difficult	less difficult	least difficult

1. If only two items are involved in a comparison, the comparative degree should be used. If three or more items are involved, the superlative degree should be used.

> POOR: *Of my two sons, the youngest is the tallest.*
> GOOD: *Of my two sons, the younger is the taller.*
>
> POOR: *Of my three sons, the younger is the taller.*
> GOOD: *Of my three sons, the youngest is the tallest.*

2. Never use both *more* and *-er* or *most* and *-est* with the same word. This is called a *double comparison* and is always incorrect. Use one form or the other, but not both.

> WRONG: *He was the most unkindest man I had ever met.*
> RIGHT: *He was the unkindest man I have ever met.*
> RIGHT: *He was the most unkind man I had ever met.*
>
> WRONG: *Yesterday was more cooler than today.*
> RIGHT: *Yesterday was cooler than today.*

3. A few adjectives are absolute and cannot be compared. The most important of these is *unique*. *Unique* means "the only one of its kind," and there can't be any more or less than that. More often than not, *unusual* is meant when *unique* is used, and *unusual* can be compared. Other absolute adjectives are *perfect, straight, round, square.*

> WRONG: *Fred Astaire was more unique than any other dancer of modern times.*
> RIGHT: *Fred Astaire was a unique dancer.*
> RIGHT: *Fred Astaire was one of the more unusual dancers of modern times.*
>
> WRONG: *Tracy played more perfect tennis than anybody else.*
> RIGHT: *Tracy played perfect tennis.*
> RIGHT: *Tracy played better tennis than any of the others.*

4. The superlative degree should be used with care so that sweeping generalizations are avoided. The use of qualifying words will tend to make the superlative degree more acceptable.

> POOR: *Abraham Lincoln was the greatest American.*
> GOOD: *Some people feel that Abraham Lincoln was the greatest American.*
> GOOD: *Abraham Lincoln was one of the greatest Americans.*
>
> POOR: *Jim Thorpe was the greatest athlete of all time.*
> GOOD: *Jim Thorpe was among the greatest athletes of all time.*
> GOOD: *A number of experts feel that Jim Thorpe was the greatest athlete of all time.*

5. Particularly in sentences that include the word *than*, care must be taken to compare similar things.

> POOR: *Sam's voice is deeper than Bill.*
> GOOD: *Sam's voice is deeper than Bill's.*
> GOOD: *Sam's voice is deeper than Bill's voice.*
>
> POOR: *The air in the country is sweeter than the city.*
> GOOD: *The air in the country is sweeter than the city's.*
> GOOD: *The air in the country is sweeter than the city's air.*

6. Particularly in certain sentences that include the word *than*, care must be taken that the meaning is clear.

> CLEAR: *That boy is fatter than I. (This sentence can mean only, "That boy is fatter than I am.")*

CLEAR:	*The chicken is tastier than the vegetables. (This sentence can mean only, "The chicken is tastier than the vegetables are.")*
UNCLEAR:	*She hates parties more than her husband. (This sentence can mean, "She hates parties more than her husband does." Or it can mean, "She hates parties more than she hates her husband.")*
UNCLEAR:	*Cats eat more canned food than mice. (This sentence can mean, "Cats eat more canned food than mice eat." Or it can mean, "Cats eat more canned food than they eat mice.")*

Notice that in some sentences of this type, the meaning you intend will affect the case of the personal pronoun.

My sister likes the cat more than I. (This sentence means, "My sister likes the cat more than I do.")

My sister likes the cat more than me. (This sentence means, "My sister likes the cat more than she likes me.")

7. Comparisons must be logical. Use the word *other* when comparing a person or thing with a group to which the person or thing belongs.

ILLOGICAL:	*Ivan is a better passer than any player on his team. (Is Ivan better than himself?)*
LOGICAL:	*Ivan is a better passer than any other player on the team.*
ILLOGICAL:	*The cheetah can run faster than any animal. (Can the cheetah run faster than a cheetah?)*
LOGICAL:	*The cheetah can run faster than any other animal.*

Exercise 12   Revise each of the following sentences so that any error in comparison, including sweeping generalization, is eliminated.

1. Satin is more smoother than silk.

_____

2. The supersonic jet is the most unique plane flying today.

_____

3. The sinking of the *Titanic* was the worst disaster in history.

_____

4. Sometimes we have to choose the least of two evils.

_____

5. The elephant's weight is greater than the whale.

_____

6. Sacramento is closer to Auburn than San Francisco.

_____

7. Chess is more complicated than any game.

_____

Modeling

After you have gone through the exercises, return to the literary model. Notice Bronowski's use of parallel structures. You should find additional sentences that use similar parallel forms:

a. Gold is the universal prize *in all countries, in all cultures, in all ages.*

b. *Gold for greed, gold for splendor, gold for adornment.* . . .

c. *Sacrificial gold, life-giving gold, barbaric gold.* . . .

d. In that phrase we become aware that gold has a physical quality that makes it singular; which can be tested or *assayed in practice,* and *characterized in theory.*

Likewise, note his use of comparison, especially in these model sentences:

e. This is a hundred times *more heavenly* than I would ever have thought!

f. A bone-ash vessel . . . is . . . brought up to a temperature much *higher* than pure gold requires.

g. It also carried a powerful symbolism, which is explicit even in the *earliest* formulae.

h. . . . Goldsmiths assayed . . . it by an acid treatment that was *less laborious* than cupellation.

When you have finished the exercises and studied the model, give your composition a final proofreading.

Peer or Self-Evaluation Guidelines

Before you prepare a final copy of your research article about gold, ask a peer or peers to read it and use the following guidelines for offering suggestions. Or use the guidelines as a means of self-evaluation.

	very well	1	2	3	4	*poorly*
1. How well does the paper demonstrate effective diction, suitable for both the topic and the audience?						
2. How well does the writer organize the research article, providing adequate parts to clarify the whole?						
3. How well does the writer use details, either by naming or describing the parts or characterizing the whole?						
4. How well does the writer use parallel structures?						
5. How well does the writer create comparisons?						

The Final Draft: Sharing

Before you prepare your final draft for the publishing stage, take into consideration your peers' suggestions and/or your self-evaluation based on the guidelines. Add a title. Then read again to check for final details. Be sure to credit sources by using any standard documentation form.

Unit 10

A Humorous Composition on Fads and Fashions

PREWRITING

Reading the Literature

From toddlers to grandmothers, we pull on blue jeans and add a T-shirt as a kind of casual uniform. Then we "dress up" those same jeans with a great shirt, blouse, sweater, or jacket. Those denim pants were not, however, always the accepted mode of dress.

The following article from *The New Yorker* suggests 1979 reactions to the then new-found popularity of blue jeans. Now, years later, they are of course even more popular. As you read to enjoy John Brooks' article, think about some fad or fashion clothing that has been—or still is—a part of your life.

A FRIENDLY PRODUCT by John Brooks

One of the major contributions of the United States to the post-war world at large—along with the computer, the copying machine, rock music, polio vaccine, and the hydrogen bomb—is the habit of wearing blue jeans. Before the 1950s, this kind of garment, noted particularly for its durability under stress, its association with the Western cowboy, and, its partisans insist, its uniquely affectionate relationship with the anatomy of the wearer, was worn, principally in the West and Southwest of the United States, by children, farmers, manual laborers when on the job, and, of course, cowboys. There were isolated exceptions—for example, artists of both sexes took to blue jeans in and around Santa Fe, New Mexico, in the 1920s and '30s, and in the late '40s the students of Bennington College adopted them as a virtual uniform, though only for wear on campus—but it was not until the 1950s, when James Dean and Marlon Brando wore jeans in movies about youth in revolt against parents and society, when John Wayne wore them in movies about untrammeled heroes in a lawless Old West, and when many schools from coast to coast gave their new symbolism a boost by banning them as inappropriate for classrooms, that jeans acquired the ideological baggage necessary to propel them to national fame.

After that, though, fame came quickly, and it was not long before young Americans—whether to express social dissent, to enjoy comfort, or to emulate their peers—had become so attached to their jeans that some hardly ever took them off. According to a jeans authority, a young man in the North Bronx with a large and indulgent family attained some sort of record by continuously wearing the same pair of jeans, even for bathing and sleeping, for over eight months. Eventually, as all the world knows, the popularity of jeans spread from cowboys and anomic youths to adult Americans of virtually every age and sociopolitical posture, conspicuously including President Carter when he was a candidate for the Presidency. Trucks containing jeans now rank as one of the three leading targets of hijackers, along with those containing liquor and cigarettes. Estimates of jeans sales in the United States vary wildly, chiefly because the line between jeans and slacks has come to be a fuzzy one. According to the most conservative figures, put out by the leading jeans manufacturer, Levi Strauss Company, of San Francisco, annual sales of jeans of all kinds in the United States by all manufacturers in 1950 stood at around 150 million pairs, and as late as 1967 at just over 200 million, while for 1977 they came to over 500 million, or considerably more than two pairs for every man, woman, and child in the country.

Overseas, jeans had to wait slightly longer for their time to come. American Western movies and the example of American servicemen from the West and Southwest stationed abroad who, as soon as the Second World War ended, changed directly from their service uniforms into blue jeans bought at post exchanges started a fad for them among Europeans in the late 1940s. But the fad remained a small one partly because of the unavailability of jeans in any quantity; in those days European customers considered jeans ersatz unless they came from the United States, while United States jeans manufacturers were inclined to be satisfied with a reliable domestic market. Being perennially short of denim, the rough, durable, naturally shrink-and-stretch cotton twill of which basic jeans are made, they were reluctant or unable to undertake overseas expansion.

Gradually, though, denim production in the United States increased, and meanwhile demand for American-made jeans became so overwhelming that in parts of Europe a black market for them developed. American jeans manufacturers began exporting their product in a serious way in the early 1960s. At first, demand was greatest in Germany, France, England, and the Benelux nations; later it spread to Italy, Spain, and Scandinavia, and eventually to Latin America and the Far East. By 1967, jeans authorities estimate, 190 million pairs of jeans were being sold annually outside the United States; of these, all but a small fraction were of local manufacture, and not imports from the United States, although American-made jeans were still so avidly sought after that some of the local products were blatant counterfeits of the leading American brands, complete with expertly faked labels. In the late 1970s, estimated jeans sales outside the United States have doubled in a decade, to 380 million pairs, of which perhaps a quarter are now made by American firms in plants abroad; the markets in Europe, Mexico, Japan, Australia, and other places have come so close to the saturation point that the fastest-growing jeans market now is probably Brazil; Princess Anne, of Great Britain, and Princess Caroline, of Monaco, have been photographed wearing jeans, and King Hussein of Jordan is reported to wear them at home in his palace; the counterfeiting of American brands is a huge international undertaking, which the leading American manufacturers combat with world-ranging security operations; Levi Strauss has sponsored and is now supervising a jeans plant in Hungary and conducting an export trade to East Germany; and in Russia, to which no American jeans are as yet commercially exported in any numbers—although the second-largest United States manufacturer, Blue Bell, announced late last year a preliminary agreement with the Soviet Union looking toward a manufacturing arrangement like Levi Strauss's with Hungary—pairs that are brought in by athletes who have visited the United States or that arrive by more devious means regularly command a price of eighty dollars or more each. All in all, it is now beyond doubt that in size and scope the rapid global spread of the habit of wearing blue jeans, however it may be explained, is an event without precedent in the history of human attire.

from *The New Yorker*

Reader Response

Humor is difficult to characterize, but we recognize it when we see or hear it. With your peers, identify and lightly underline the humorous elements in Brooks' essay. Discuss what makes the humor work.

Next, on your own, think about a current craze or fashion fad. You may want to update Brooks' ideas about blue jeans or turn to some other item, such as T-shirts, jogging shoes, gold neck chains, scents, hairstyles, leather skirts and slacks, designer labels, and so on. In your response journal, write about some such popular fashion. As a guide, you may want to address questions such as these:

a. Why is this item important?

b. Why has it become so popular?

c. How does this fashion craze or fad fit in the larger setting?

As you write, look for opportunities to include irony and humor, similar, perhaps, to that of Brooks.

Active Reading

Reread "A Friendly Product." Study the sentences Brooks uses. Some are short and simple; some are long but still simple. Others are complex; many are compound-complex. See if you can identify by type each of the sentences in "A Friendly Product." Label them in the margin. What generalizations can you make about Brooks' sentence variety?

Studying Model Writing Techniques

Sentence Variety: Simple, Compound, and Complex Sentences

REMEMBER! All sorts of choices are open to you in the kinds of words and sentences you use to express yourself.

A variety of sentence forms is available to you in your writing. By making choices among these forms, you can add interest and clarity to your writing.

Here are the choices available to you.

You can write simple sentences, consisting of one main clause.

Millions died.
The great plague took millions of lives.
Millions of people, stricken by the plague, suffered terribly and died.

You can write compound sentences, consisting of two main clauses connected by *and*, *or*, *but*, or a semicolon. (Note that the compound sentences use a comma between the two independent clauses unless the sentences are very short.)

The dam burst *and* the valley was flooded.

The dam burst; the valley was flooded.

You were away having a good time, *and* I was here bored and lonely.

I may not succeed *but* I will try.

The road ahead was long and rough, *but* it was by now too late to turn back.

Take it or leave it. (*You* is understood as the subject of both clauses: You take it or you leave it.)

You can thoughtlessly spend the money now, or you can wisely put it in the bank for important future needs.

You can write complex sentences, consisting of one main clause and one or more subordinate clauses.

After she had spoken, everyone was silent.

It is hard to understand our energy difficulties *because energy is all about us in the forms of gravity, magnetism, heat, light, moving air, and moving water.*

If it doesn't rain tomorrow, the roads will be jammed with cars.

Exercise 1   Identify the following Brooks sentences, or parts of sentences, by type. Note that some may be both compound and complex.

_____ **1.** Overseas, jeans had to wait slightly longer for their time to come.

_____ **2.** According to a jeans authority, a young man in the North Bronx with a large and indulgent family attained some sort of record by continuously wearing the same pair of jeans, even for bathing and sleeping, for over eight months.

_____ **3.** Eventually, as all the world knows, the popularity of jeans spread from cowboys and anomic youths to adult Americans of virtually every age and sociopolitical posture, conspicuously including President Carter when he was a candidate for the Presidency.

_____ **4.** After that, though, fame came quickly, and it was not long before young Americans—whether to express social dissent, to enjoy comfort, or to emulate their peers—had become so attached to their jeans that some hardly every took them off.

_____ **5.** All in all, it is now beyond doubt that in size and scope the rapid global spread of the habit of wearing blue jeans, however it may be explained, is an event without precedent in the history of human attire.

Exercise 2 Change each pair of simple sentences into a compound sentence. Depending on the meaning you want, you can use *and*, *but*, or *or*. You can also use a semicolon.

1. Spring came. The birds flew north.

_____

2. Cotton is soft. Synthetics are not.

_____

3. She was a fine tennis player. She was a good all-around athlete.

_____

_____

4. The day was bitter cold. He wore no coat.

_____

_____

5. The dish can be eaten hot. It can be served cold.

_____

_____

6. For my vacation I may go to the shore. I may just stay here and rest.

_____

_____

7. The outfit is comfortable. It is not suitable for cooler weather.

_____

_____

8. Mars is closer. Jupiter appears brighter.

_____

_____

9. Fortunes are made in real-estate speculation. Fortunes are lost in real-estate speculation.

_____

_____

10. The cold, gray, depressing winter was almost over. Everyone cheered up.

_____

_____

Exercise 3   Change each of the following compound sentences into two simple sentences.

1. James Watt did not actually invent the steam engine, but he did improve it greatly.

_____

_____

2. We must hurry, or we'll miss the bus.

_____

_____

3. A rifle cracked, and the deer fell dead.

_____

_____

4. We have a few more miles to go; then we'll eat.

_____

_____

5. With a roar and a tremble, the giant plane began its run down the strip, gathering speed with every thrust of its engines, and before we knew it, we were airborne.

_____

_____

_____

6. The children wanted to play touch football, but they couldn't find a ball.

_____

_____

7. It was a marvelously suspenseful book and I couldn't put it down.

_____

_____

8. You can brown the meat in butter, or you can brown it in vegetable oil.

_____

_____

9. The hours ticked away but the phone did not ring.

_____

_____

10. The application form was handed to him; he dreaded the task of filling it out.

_____

_____

Exercise 4   Change each of the following complex sentences into two simple sentences. As examples, the first two are done for you.

1. The residents have to boil their water because it is contaminated.

   The residents have to boil their water. It is contaminated.

2. If this is gold, our fortunes are made.

   This is gold. Our fortunes are made.

3. After I eat breakfast, I brush my teeth.

4. When the alarm went off, the fire fighters sprang into action.

5. When the movie ended, the audience began to applaud.

6. Joan is engaged to a young man who is from Louisville.

7. When the car went out of control, it struck a pole.

8. A plant that has large yellow flowers is growing in the garden.

9. The law was passed, although many thought it to be a bad one.

10. On the wall hung a beautiful painting that was done by Monet.

Exercise 5   Change each of the following pairs of simple sentences into complex sentences. Use the connecting word given in brackets. The first is done for you as an example.

1. The building was well constructed. It withstood the earthquake [*which*]

   The building, which was well constructed, withstood the earthquake.

2. She has many strong emotions. She hides them from others. [*which*]

3. They selected wallpaper. It was bright red. [*that*]

4. He was short of money. He tried to get a loan. [*because*]

_____

_____

5. The band finished playing. We sat and enjoyed the night air. [*after*]

_____

_____

6. The apples weren't ripe. We ate them anyway. [*although*]

_____

_____

7. The new neighbors were polite and quiet. Everyone welcomed them. [*since*]

_____

_____

8. Dawn breaks. The birds begin to sing. [*when*]

_____

_____

9. The tide grew steadily higher. The water reached the seawall. [*until*]

_____

_____

10. There are no problems. Life is dull. [*when*]

_____

_____

Exercise 6   Add words of your own to make each of the simple sentences into a compound sentence. Try to use each of the connectives—*and*, *but*, *or*, semicolon (*;*)—at least once. The first two are done for you as examples.

1. The lights went out.

The lights went out; the room was plunged into darkness.

2. The river can be crossed by ferry.

The river can be crossed by ferry, or one can use the bridge.

3. Report to the office by 9:00 A.M.

_____

_____

4. There are fine beaches on our Atlantic coast.

_____

5. Many presents lay on the table.

6. The neighbor played his stereo at top volume.

7. There were long lines at every window in the bank.

8. White-water canoeing is a thrilling adventure.

9. The game began.

10. The birds have eaten nearly all the fruit off the cherry tree.

Exercise 7   Add words of your own to make each of the following simple sentences into a complex sentence. You will need to make use of such connecting words as *who, which, that, because, if, although, after, until, when, since, before*. The first two sentences have been done for you as examples.

1. The bus was jammed with people.

Although the bus was jammed with people, everyone was patient and polite.

2. In the window was a lovely bracelet.

In the window was a lovely bracelet, which she could not afford to buy.

3. The suitcase was made of the finest leather.

4. We soaked in the warm sun.

5. Gray clouds hung in the sky.

_____

_____

6. The clown stepped into the spotlight.

_____

_____

7. Smoking is hazardous to the health.

_____

_____

8. We heard the bicycle in the driveway.

_____

_____

9. Spanish is the language of many countries.

_____

_____

10. Horses grazed in the fields.

_____

COMPUTER HINT

Although style checkers will measure lengths of sentences and, in most cases, provide a "readability level," do not be deceived by these somewhat gimmicky tools. While certainly sentence length is a viable means by which to measure sentence variety, it is only one means. Style checkers will not determine sentence type, sentence structure, sentence modifiers, or sentence parts.

RESPONSE

Modeling

Study the sentences you wrote in your response journal about a fashion craze or fad. Even though you were writing informally, you probably included at least two types of sentences. Do you see ways in which you could revise certain sentences, similar to those in the exercises above, that would improve your sentence variety? Remember, however, that a variety of types alone will not guarantee good sentence variety. You will also vary sentences by length, by modifiers, by structure—all aspects you've already studied.

Writing

Skim through your journal notes. Your task now is to write a humorous composition on fads and fashions. Although you may choose and develop your own subject, you may want to follow the suggestions here:

In your first paragraph, you will probably want to establish the identity and importance of the item you are writing about. You can give a few key descriptive details and examples that suggest the appearance and widespread use of the item. Here is an illustration:

> Once they were called sneakers and consisted of a soft canvas top with ground-gripping rubber soles. Now they are the end product of advanced engineering and technology along with fashion design, specialized for every sport, and approved for social wear. They go by such names as Puma, Converse, and Adidas. They have become a cult. The corporation director is as likely to attend a board meeting wearing this latest craze of footwear as is my sixty-year-old neighbor huffing and puffing his way through his daily jogging stint.

Your second and third paragraphs can be devoted to reasons explaining why so many people have taken to the fad. Before writing, think of as many different kinds of reasons as you can. What role is played by the following considerations: personal comfort, economy, status seeking, health, self-expression, rebellion, and conformity? From the many reasons that will occur to you, choose a few, perhaps only two, that you will emphasize in these two paragraphs.

In your fourth and concluding paragraph, you may wish to broaden your focus and view the particular fad you have been writing about as part of a larger setting. For example, you may wish to explain the fad as one aspect of a general life-style or sociological trend, such as sexual equality or individual liberation or social protest. Or you may wish to discuss the general nature of such fads and crazes. Here you may find it useful to refer to fads of the ancient and more recent past: the binding of women's feet in China, the wearing of elaborate wigs in the eighteenth century, the emphasis on long hair or on the miniskirt of the 1960s. What does it all mean?

In writing this composition, try to make use of some of the opportunities you will have to add the sparkle of irony and humor. One way to achieve humor or irony is by the

> ## COMPUTER HINT
>
> If your software and hardware have the capability, develop an illustration for your paper. Perhaps you can scan a photograph to incorporate within your text. Perhaps you can incorporate your own computer-produced sketch. Perhaps you can do a graphics design that satirizes your topic. Such a creative touch enhances reader interest.

use of deliberate exaggeration. For example, the writer of the passage on blue jeans uses exaggeration in equating jeans and rock music in importance with the hydrogen bomb and polio vaccine. Another way to achieve humor is by presenting facts that are incredible or incongruous, such as the facts that blue jeans were given a boost when they were banned from classrooms, that blue jeans are on a par with liquor and cigarettes as an object for hijackers, and that blue jeans cost eighty dollars in Russia.

REVISION

Now that you have finished the first draft of your humorous composition about fads and fashions, you are ready to revise. In the revision process, we will focus on organization, chains of meaning, and proofreading details. Use the materials as a model for your own revision process.

Checking Organization

Causes and Effects; Reasons and Results

REMEMBER! Organized thinking is essential in composition writing.

An important skill of organization is the ability to recognize how ideas are related as **causes** and **effects** or as **reasons** and **results.** These exercises will help train you to be more efficient in cause-effect and reason-result thinking.

For instance, look at the following pairs of words. If you see a cause-effect or reason-result relationship between the words in each pair, write "yes" in the space provided. If you don't see a cause-effect or reason-result relationship, write "no."

_____ *a.* tornado—destruction

_____ *b.* tomato—orange

_____ *c.* worry—headache

If you wrote "yes" for item *a*, you were right. A tornado will, of course, cause or result in destruction. If you wrote "no" for *b*, you were right because no cause-effect or reason-result relationship is suggested between tomato and orange. If you wrote "yes" for *c*, you were right. Worry is a form of stress that may result in a headache.

Exercise 8   Brooks uses a number of causes and effects, reasons and results in his humorous essay on blue jeans. See if you can locate at least five of them and paraphrase the ideas. One is done for you.

1. *Because movie stars wore blue jeans, more people accepted the garments.*

2. _____

_____

3. _____

_____

4. _____

_____

5. _____

_____

Exercise 9 Look at the following pairs of words. If you see a cause-effect or reason-result relationship between the words in each pair, write "yes" in the space provided. If you don't see a cause-effect or reason-result relationship, write "no" in the space provided.

_____ **1.** bad—bounce

_____ **2.** practice—improvement

_____ **3.** nutrition—health

_____ **4.** trouble—peace

_____ **5.** friction—heat

_____ **6.** haste—waste

_____ **7.** halt—stop

_____ **8.** insecurity—shyness

_____ **9.** boredom—yawning

_____ **10.** fireworks—injury

_____ **11.** box—fruit

_____ **12.** jump—run

_____ **13.** height—dizziness

_____ **14.** love—consideration

_____ **15.** honesty—trust

Exercise 10 The words in column I list possible causes or reasons. The words in column II list in scrambled order effects or results. Alongside each word in column I, write the word from column II that forms the best cause-effect or reason-result match.

Column I		_Column II_
1. humidity	_____	rejoicing
2. uncertainty	_____	fever
3. victory	_____	punishment
4. infection	_____	perspiration
5. bacteria	_____	laughter
6. stumble	_____	fear
7. joke	_____	hesitation
8. danger	_____	fall
9. fertility	_____	decay
10. crime	_____	crops

Exercise 11 Try an exercise in more original cause-effect or reason-result thinking. Here is a list of possible effects or results. In the space following each, give two possible causes or reasons. The first is done for you as an example.

1. Dental cavities

Eating too many sweets _____

Poor brushing habits _____

2. Feeling depressed

_____

_____

3. Running out of money

_____

_____

4. Enjoying a party

_____

_____

5. Moving to another state

_____

_____

6. Having a hoarse voice

_____

_____

7. The car won't start.

_____

_____

8. Wanting a pet cat

_____

_____

9. A child runs away from home.

_____

_____

10. The price of coffee goes up.

_____

_____

11. Someone decides to become a doctor.

_____

_____

12. No traffic on the roads

_____

_____

13. A person loses his or her job.

_____

_____

14. Electric power goes out.

_____

_____

15. Disaster movies are the most popular.

_____

_____

Modeling

Examine the draft of your humorous essay on a fashion craze or fad. Can your reader readily identify causes, effects, reasons, and results? Is the paper organized in such a way to clarify those relationships? If possible, ask a peer or peers to read your paper and respond to these questions. Revise as necessary.

Checking Chains of Meaning

Cause-Effect; Reason-Result

REMEMBER! In composition writing, sentences are not individual or isolated. Instead, the thought is carried along from sentence to sentence in a chain of meaning.

The most important skill of composition that you have begun to learn in this book is the development of a single idea in a sequence of sentences. Without this skill, there is simply no composition.

Through development, the single idea is made clearer and more alive, explained better, made more complete and convincing. You have learned a number of thought forms through which development can take place.

In this final unit, you will learn what in some ways may be the most important thought form: statements of cause and effect or reason and result. This is the thought form that attempts to answer the question, "Why?" This is the thought form we use when we make big decisions, when we try to understand how to improve our own lives, to solve the problems of the world we live in, to explain history, to understand nature.

Exercise 12 The thought form of the following sentence sequences is cause-effect or reason-result. In the spaces following each sequence, briefly state in your own words the cause or reason and the effect or result. The first sequence has been done for you as an example.

1. In the last three months, there have been fewer fatal accidents on the roads. This improvement has been attributed to the lower speed limits.

CAUSE OR REASON: _lower speed limits_

EFFECT OR RESULT: _fewer fatal accidents_

2. The wheat crop this past season was abundant. In the stores, the price of bread has gone down.

CAUSE OR REASON: _____

EFFECT OR RESULT: _____

3. The child has never brushed her teeth. Her mouth is full of cavities.

CAUSE OR REASON: _____

EFFECT OR RESULT: _____

4. Inferior materials were used in the original construction. Now the roads are in need of constant repair.

CAUSE OR REASON: _____

EFFECT OR RESULT: _____

5. I was late for my appointment. An accident on the expressway stalled traffic.

CAUSE OR REASON: _____

EFFECT OR RESULT: _____

6. He has gone on a diet. All his clothes were getting too tight.

CAUSE OR REASON: _____

EFFECT OR RESULT: _____

7. The weather was perfect for the holiday weekend. The beaches were jammed.

CAUSE OR REASON: _____

EFFECT OR RESULT: _____

8. Jean was happier than ever. She loved her new job.

CAUSE OR REASON: _____

EFFECT OR RESULT: _____

9. George decided to drop out of school for a year. He wanted time to think about his future.

CAUSE OR REASON: _____

EFFECT OR RESULT: _____

10. George decided to drop out of school for a year. His father was in a rage about it.

CAUSE OR REASON: _____

EFFECT OR RESULT: _____

11. The company had lost its two largest accounts. It was on the verge of bankruptcy.

CAUSE OR REASON: _____

EFFECT OR RESULT: _____

12. The company has lost its two largest accounts. A competitor had cut prices.

CAUSE OR REASON: _____

EFFECT OR RESULT: _____

13. She felt depressed and lonely. She had not heard from Harry in two weeks.

CAUSE OR REASON: _____

EFFECT OR RESULT: _____

14. She had not heard from Harry in two weeks. He might be ill.

CAUSE OR REASON: _____

EFFECT OR RESULT: _____

15. Some people place great stress on status symbols. They wear diamonds and drive Cadillacs.

CAUSE OR REASON: _____

EFFECT OR RESULT: _____

16. The air quality was bad. People had tearing eyes and running noses.

CAUSE OR REASON: _____

EFFECT OR RESULT: _____

17. Anna hated crowds and noise. She insisted on living in a rural area.

CAUSE OR REASON: _____

EFFECT OR RESULT: _____

18. Anna insisted on living in a rural area. Her husband had to travel an hour and a half to get to work.

CAUSE OR REASON: _____

EFFECT OR RESULT: _____

19. The bank installed bullet-proof glass windows. The tellers felt more secure.

CAUSE OR REASON: _____

EFFECT OR RESULT: _____

20. The bank installed bullet-proof glass windows. It had been held up three times in three weeks.

CAUSE OR REASON: _____

EFFECT OR RESULT: _____

Exercise 13 Here are twenty simple statements. Look at each, and think of a cause or reason or an effect or result that you can tie in with each statement. Then write a sequence of two sentences, using the given idea and your own related cause, effect, reason, or result.

You can change the wording of each given statement in any way you choose. The first is done for you as an example.

1. The baby is crying.

   The baby must be teething. She has been crying all night.

2. You see a certain movie.

3. A hurricane strikes.

4. A football star is injured.

5. A couple quarrels.

6. You go to the doctor.

7. You call the police.

8. It is a hot, humid day.

9. A disarmament treaty is signed.

10. A window is broken.

_____

_____

_____

11. Someone laughs and laughs.

_____

_____

12. A large crowd gathers.

_____

_____

_____

13. Martin goes shopping.

_____

_____

_____

14. You are stung by a bee.

_____

_____

15. Someone tears a letter into small pieces.

_____

_____

_____

16. The summer vacation begins.

_____

_____

_____

17. You cast a vote for your candidate for president.

_____

_____

_____

18. Someone breaks a mirror.

_____

_____

19. Someone buys a car phone.

_____

_____

_____

20. The sink is piled with dirty dishes.

_____

_____

_____

Modeling

Return to your work in progress and look for the chains of meaning that clarify, explain, or make your ideas more complete and convincing. Do you help your reader follow your thought forms? Ask a peer or peers for their response. Based on their advice and on the exercises you have done, make any necessary revisions to your humorous essay.

Proofreading

As you proofread for errors in spelling and punctuation, you should take special note of a common error emphasized for your attention: verb tenses. The exercises that follow will help you to recognize and avoid this error in your writing.

Tenses: Present, Past, Present Perfect

Past events can be told using the past tense of verbs.

> GOOD: _He_ mounted _the steps to the guillotine. A blindfold_ was placed _over his eyes. The mob_ shouted, _"Off with his head!" He_ knelt _below the poised knife. The blade_ dropped.

Sometimes, for dramatic effect, past events are told in the present tense.

> GOOD: _He_ mounts _the steps of the guillotine. A blindfold_ is placed _over his eyes. The mob_ shouts, _"Off with his head!" He_ kneels _below the poised knife. The blade_ drops.

However, you must stick consistently to the tense you have chosen. It is poor writing to shift illogically back and forth between tenses.

> POOR: _He_ mounted _the steps to the guillotine. A blindfold_ is placed _over his eyes. The mob_ shouted, _"Off with his head!" He_ kneels _below the guillotine. The blade_ dropped.

Here are two more examples of sentence sequences in which the writing shifts tenses unnecessarily. Notice that you can correct the error either by making the verbs consistently present tense or past tense.

> POOR: _The dog_ approaches _me. He_ wags _his tail. Then he_ began _to bark. He_ snarled _and_ snapped.
>
> GOOD: _The dog_ approaches _me. He_ wags _his tail. Then he_ begins _to bark. He_ snarls _and_ snaps.
>
> GOOD: _The dog_ approached _me. He_ wagged _his tail. Then he_ began _to bark. He_ snarled _and_ snapped.

POOR:	At the head of the parade was a marching band. The clowns followed. Then a line of swaying elephants comes along. The lion cages bring up the rear.
GOOD:	At the head of the parade was a marching band. The clowns followed. Then a line of swaying elephants came along. The lion cages brought up the rear.
GOOD:	At the head of the parade is a marching band. The clowns follow. Then a line of swaying elephants comes along. The lion cages bring up the rear.

When you are writing in the past tense, be especially careful with such verbs as *used, hoped, liked, waved* when they are followed by the word *to*. The tendency is to leave out the *d* in the verb. Be especially careful with *used to*!

WRONG:	They use to go for a stroll in the park.
RIGHT:	They used to go for a stroll in the park.

WRONG:	The jockey hope to win the last race.
RIGHT:	The jockey hoped to win the last race.

WRONG:	The child like to be rocked in his cradle.
RIGHT:	The child liked to be rocked in his cradle.

WRONG:	The famous star wave to her admiring fans.
RIGHT:	The famous star waved to her admiring fans.

Look at the following sentence:

The astronomer proved that the earth revolved around the sun.

This sentence may seem to be correct because both verbs are in the past tense. However, note that the earth does not revolve around the sun only in the past, when the astronomer proved it. The earth always revolves around the sun. It is a truth that always exists. To describe an action that is always true, use the present tense, even if a verb in the past tense precedes the statement.

WRONG:	The astronomer proved that the earth revolved around the sun.
RIGHT:	The astronomer proved that the earth revolves around the sun.

WRONG:	The girl did not know what courtesy meant.
RIGHT:	The girl did not know what courtesy means.

WRONG:	Scientists realized that Hawaii was an above-water part of a mostly underwater mountain chain.
RIGHT:	Scientists realized that Hawaii is an above-water part of a mostly underwater mountain chain.

WRONG:	The student did not know what the word indigenous meant.
RIGHT:	The student did not know what the word indigenous means.

Look at these two sentences:

George *became* a dentist ten years ago. (*became*—past tense)
George *is* a dentist now. (*is*—present tense)

These two sentences cover a time span that began in the past and continues to the present. We can combine these two sentences and cover the whole time span with one verb.

George *has been* a dentist for ten years.

The verb *has been* is in the present perfect tense. The present perfect tense is used to cover a time span that began in the past and has continued to the present.

WRONG: *It is raining steadily for four weeks.*
RIGHT: *It has rained steadily for four weeks.*

WRONG: *I live here for the last ten years.*
WRONG: *I lived here for the last ten years.*
RIGHT: *I have lived here for the last ten years.*

WRONG: *I did not receive my check yet.*
RIGHT: *I have not received my check yet.*

WRONG: *The pothole is here for a month.*
RIGHT: *The pothole has been here for a month.*

Exercise 14 Of the following sentences, eight contain an error in tense. Two are correct. Revise the incorrect sentences to eliminate the error. Leave the others alone.

1. The oak tree has stood on this spot for the last hundred years.

_____

_____

2. The researcher discovered the virus that caused measles.

_____

_____

3. The king descended from his throne, and the courtiers bow and make a path for him.

_____

_____

4. Some football stars use to play without a helmet.

_____

_____

5. We did not have our vacation yet.

_____

_____

6. The class learned that the square root of nine is three.

_____

_____

7. Since it was first organized years ago with high hopes, the United Nations faced many unsolvable problems.

_____

_____

8. They use to grow vegetables, but now they grow only flowers in their garden.

_____

_____

9. When the lost child was finally found, the mother first hugs and kisses it and then smacked it for running away.

_____

_____

_____

10. Our primitive ancestors did not understand what earthquakes were, and they thought the gods were angry.

_____

_____

Tenses: Past Perfect

Look at these two sentences. What is the difference in meaning?

When they arrived, I left.
When they arrived, I had left.

The writer has a choice between these two sentences, depending on the meaning he or she wishes to express. In the first sentence, both verbs are in the past tense. The two actions (_arriving_ and _leaving_) occurred at the same time. The meaning is, "I passed them by as they arrived and I was leaving."

In the second sentence, the first verb (_arrived_) is in the past tense. The second verb (_had left_) is in the past perfect tense, which is used to show an action that occurred before another past action. The meaning of this sentence is, "I was gone well before they showed up."

Use the past perfect tense to express action that happened in the past before another past action.

In the following sentence, the writer has no choice. Why?

They arrived after I had left.

The past perfect must be used for past action that clearly occurred before another past action. In this sentence, the word _after_ requires use of the past perfect.

Exercise 15   In each sentence, make the necessary change of a verb to the past perfect tense.

1. The baby was crying for an hour before anyone heard anything.

_____

2. They already ordered dinner before we arrived at the table.

_____

3. The accident occurred because the car's brakes failed.

_____

4. Martin discovered to his dismay that he forgot to take his wallet with him.

_____

5. By the time you called, I already made another date.

_____

6. Frank told me he met my father downtown earlier in the day.

_____

7. The announcer stated that a new world's record was set.

_____

8. After they were on the road for an hour, they wondered whether they closed the windows and locked the door of the house.

_____

_____

9. The bank was robbed ten minutes after I left it.

_____

10. The visitors learned that George Washington slept in the same bed.

_____

_____

Modeling

After you have gone through the exercises, return to the literary model. Notice Brooks' use of verb tenses. Initially, most are in the simple past tense: _were, worn, took, adopted, gave, acquired_, etc. Can you identify other tenses and determine why Brooks uses them? Consider:

a. . . . It was not long before young Americans . . . _had become_ so attached to their jeans. . . . (past perfect tense)

b. Trucks containing jeans now _rank_ as one of the three leading targets of hijackers. . . . (present tense)

c. . . . Estimated jeans sales outside the United States _have doubled_ in a decade. . . . (present perfect tense)

d. . . . Levi Strauss _has sponsored_ and is now supervising a jeans plant in Hungary. . . . (present perfect tense)

When you have finished the exercises and studied the model, give your essay a final proofreading.

Peer or Self-Evaluation Guidelines

Before you prepare a final copy of your humorous essay about some fashion craze or fad, ask a peer or peers to read it and use the following guidelines for offering suggestions. Or use the guidelines as a means of self-evaluation.

	very well	1	2	3	4	poorly
1. How well does the essay demonstrate sentence variety in terms of a good combination of simple, compound, and complex sentences?						
2. How well does the writer organize causes and effects, reasons and results?						
3. How well does the writer incorporate chains of meaning to clarify cause-effect and/or reason-result?						
4. How well does the essay demonstrate accurate use of verb tenses?						

The Final Draft: Sharing

Before you prepare your final draft for the publishing stage, take into consideration your peers' suggestions and/or your self-evaluation based on the guidelines above. Add a title. Then read again to check for final details.

> ### COMPUTER HINT
>
> Now that you and your classmates have completed this course work, choose and compile your best works in a literary magazine. The choices may be made by the entire group, by small groups, or by individuals. You will be able to incorporate easily any last-minute revisions you or your peers suggest. And as a group, you can quickly produce a camera-ready copy of the completed magazine. Use a computer graphics program to design a cover; you may also choose to incorporate graphics throughout the magazine to separate groups of works or to add interest. Be sure to share your publication with classmates, the school library, and others who express interest. You've worked hard. You deserve the credit!

Index

phrases, 10, 17, 18, 93–94, 115–116, 140–141, 153–154
picture-making words, 3–6
plagiarism, 163, 164
predicate, 30, 91, 94–95
predicate nominative, 125
prewriting, v, 1–6, 15–20, 31–37, 50–55, 69–75, 90–98, 113–117, 130–143, 156–162, 177–186
pronouns, 42–44, 126–128; case, 124–126; kinds of, 62–67; possessive form of, 86–88; reference of, 65–67
proofreading, 10–13, 25–30, 44–49, 62–68, 83–88, 105–112, 124–129, 151–155, 170–176, 196–201

reading,
active, 3, 17, 32, 52, 71, 91, 115, 134, 158–159, 179
reasons-results, 188–190, 191–196
redundancy,
avoiding, 13
repetition, 42–44, 142–143
research article, 156–176
response, 4, 6–7, 20–21, 37–38, 56–57, 75–77, 98–101, 117–118, 143–144, 162–164, 186–188
response,
reader, 2–3, 17, 32, 52, 71, 91, 114, 134, 158, 179
revision, v, 7–14, 21–30, 38, 57–68, 77–88, 101–112, 118–129, 144–155, 164–176, 188–201
rhythm, 91

semicolon, 13, 27–28, 180, 181, 184
sentence, 10–12, 17–19, 27; complex, 179–186; compound, 27–29, 179–186; fragments, 10–12, 13;

run-on, 27–29; stringy, 137–139; types of, 52–55; variety, 17–19, 20, 52–55, 56, 91–98, 115–117, 134–143, 179–186
similarity and sameness, 59–62
specific words/phrases, 21–22
spelling, 105–112
step-by-step, 103–105
style, 3, 91, 144, 163
subject,
of a sentence, 17, 18, 30, 45–46, 91–94, 115, 125, 140; of a paper (see "topic")
synonyms, 32–37, 159

thesaurus, 15, 33, 37, 159
topic, 3, 37, 144, 163, 164
topic sentence, 99
transition, 8–10, 23–25, 42–43, 59 (see also "chains of meaning"); adverb, 28; sentence, 100, 118

unity, 7–8, 71–75

verbs, 30, 45, 91, 94–95, 115, 140; tenses, 196–201; shift in tense, 196
voice, 53

whole and parts, 145–146, 147–151, 164–165, 165–170
wordiness, 25–27
writing, 6–7, 20–21, 37, 56–57, 76–77, 99–101, 118, 144, 163–164, 187–188
writing process (see "prewriting," "writing," "revision," and "proofreading")